get
CRAFTY

HIP HOME EC

get

CRAFTY

JEAN RAILLA

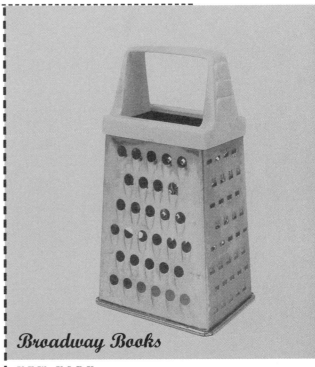

Broadway Books

NEW YORK

BROADWAY

GET CRAFTY. Copyright © 2004 by Jean Railla. All rights reserved.
No part of this book may be reproduced or transmitted in any form or by
any means, electronic or mechanical, including photocopying, recording,
or by any information storage and retrieval system, without written
permission from the publisher. For information, address Broadway Books,
a division of Random House, Inc.

PRINTED IN THE UNITED STATES OF AMERICA

BROADWAY BOOKS and its logo, a letter B bisected on the diagonal,
are trademarks of Random House, Inc.

Visit our website at www.broadwaybooks.com

First edition published 2004.

Library of Congress Cataloging-in-Publication Data
Railla, Jean,
    Get crafty : hip home ec / Jean Railla.
        p.   cm.
    1. Home economics.   2. Handicraft.   3. Cookery.   I. Title.
TX147.R25 2004
640—dc22   2003069612

ISBN 0-7679-1720-0

10 9 8 7 6 5 4 3 2 1

This book is dedicated to the Craftistas

Contents

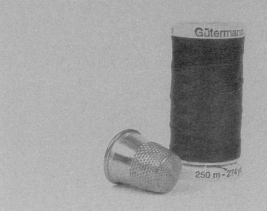

Acknowledgments

When I began this book, I was pregnant and it was winter. I finished in the fall, with my four-month-old baby boy by my side. On Mondays, Sydney and I go to "Mommy and Me" yoga. At the end of class, the teacher goes around the room thanking each baby by name for sharing the time with her and helping to create a nice experience. I'd like to do the same with all the people who helped make this book.

Thank you, Sydney Slingsby Railla-Duncombe, for being my companion throughout this entire process.

Thank you, Claudia Cross. You are a great agent and I am honored that you represent me. Thank you, Kris Puopolo and everyone at Broadway Books for making *Get Crafty* possible. Thank you, my yellow scribblers at the Writers Room.

Thank you, Kate Kirtz, for baking endless batches of madeleines and testing all the recipes, and for inspiring me with your creativity and honesty. Thank you, Tobi Armstrong, for making a last-minute bikini and sharing your punk rock knitting technique.

Thank you to everyone I interviewed and those who contributed recipes and ideas. In particular, I'd like to thank Cynthia, Clare Crespo, Amanda Cole, Susan Stars, Lisa Devo, Elain Cohen, and Ann Faison. From Glitter, I'd like to thank every single lady, but especially Chris, Amy, Janet, Becca, Susan, Suzanne, Tasha, Marisol, Elizabeth, Kari, Amy, Betsy, and Tracy.

Thank you, Caroline Sheperd, for contributing your photos to this book.

Thank you, Gayle Forman and Mary Bahr, for being such excellent readers.

Thank you, Karen Steinberg, for a great education.

Thank you to my writer's group: Dan Pinney, Kimberly Forrest, Bill Dickey, and Fiona Schaeffer. Your support made all the difference in the world.

Thank you, Maryellen Strautmanis and Sofia Contreras, for taking care of Sydney while I put the finishing touches on this book.

Thank you, Mom, for lending me your recipes. And thank you for all those years of fresh-squeezed orange juice.

Thank you to the other moms in my life: Sally Duncombe, Evelyn Garfinkle, Nancy Fairly, and Bella Mirabella.

Thank you, Meme, for teaching me the joy of cooking.

Thank you, Virginia Prescott, Dawn Avery, Tania Mara Miller, Ethan Lipton, Melinda Simon, and Emma Fairly, for your friendship.

Thank you, Laura Aviva, for being my compañera for the past twenty years.

Thank you, Debbie Stoller. Without you, *Get Crafty* would never have existed.

Finally, thank you, Steve Duncombe, for being my husband, my editor, my lover, and my best friend. Thank you for your commitment to constantly crafting our life together.

Introduction:

DOMESTIC ME

"Dear *Ms. Magazine*" was how I began my first real writing assignment. It was a letter to the editor of the quintessential second-wave feminist journal. I was thirteen and already angry; the Catholic school I attended required uniforms for girls, but not boys. Girls, declared the administration, couldn't handle the peer pressure of dressing themselves and boys shouldn't be made to suffer because of our weakness. Because I was young, my protests were shrugged off as teenage impertinence by both my parents and the school. But the rule was clearly unfair and I desperately wanted to be heard.

Ms. published my letter. Seeing it in print gave me the validation I was looking for, cementing my lifelong passion for feminism. Sitting in my suburban home in the San Fernando Valley, listening to the punk band X and leafing through my mom's back issues of *Ms.*, I dreamed of a better life—a world without ugly polyester uniforms or afternoon detention, where the women were all superstars and wore beautiful outfits, were taken seriously and maybe even revered. I promised myself I'd become a feminist warrior; I would never marry, never be tied down to keeping a home, and never find myself changing dirty diapers.

Even with this newfound politicization, I still pursued my little craft projects. I made and designed my own T-shirts, experimented with kitchen concoctions like apricot-yogurt-nutmeg smoothies, and continued with the funny "art" projects I had learned in Girl Scouts: sculptures made from dried macaroni and spray-painted gold, Popsicle-stick cabins, and jean jackets with badges and patches sewn all over them. I saw nothing contradictory about my passion for feminism and my love of crafty projects. My desire to be an influential woman and my enjoyment of crafts seemed to coexist in peaceful harmony.

As I got older, though, I grew less and less interested in the domestic arts. Consequently, I never pursued my grandmother when she offered to share her baking secrets with me, and I shrugged off my mother's attempts to teach me how to clean or do housework. I soon began to think of sewing and crafts as a waste of time; they were things that "other" women like my mother and grandmother did, but not an up-and-coming bohemian like me.

My disdain for all things domestic only increased throughout my college years. I was a women's studies major at UCLA in the early 1990s, and my professors, mostly second-wave feminists, perceived the home and its accompanying activities as something from which women needed to free themselves. The subtext was that housework and the domestic arts were drudgery—work done by women who didn't know better. Smart, enlightened women became writers, thinkers; they became important, *like men.* They didn't have time for silly things like cooking, sewing, knitting, or cleaning. Of course, there were a few exceptions to this rule, post-modern feminists who were questioning the liberal ideology of the more mainstream professors, but for the most part, the logic of the day was work/career is good; home/domesticity is bad.

And this all made sense to me. I spent most of my twenties

defining myself as a feminist not by what I did, but what I *didn't* do. I didn't keep house. I didn't get married. I didn't cook very often. I didn't knit or sew.

Then, at age twenty-eight, I crashed. Sure, I had built a successful career as a Web site producer in New York City. I was living the life I was supposed to live as a contemporary woman: I paid my own rent, went out almost every night, slept with whomever I wanted, and was utterly undomestic. Yet there was something missing. Along with the fulfilling job and active social life, I had credit card debt, a crappy apartment, bad eating habits, worse boyfriend choices, and no real clue as to how to be a grown-up.

In my attempts to avoid domestic entrapment, I had unwittingly become vulnerable and a bit childish; while I could pay the bills, I didn't have a sustainable lifestyle. In not wanting to be a typical woman, I was waiting for someone else to come clean the house and make me feel better. But that person never showed up.

When a particularly painful bout of migraines left me debilitated for over a week, I took it as a sign that my life had to change. I began reevaluating who I was and what I wanted, including many of the things that I had always dismissed. Were cooking, crafts, and keeping house things that would limit my life? I had always thought so, but living like a slob wasn't very enjoyable. What did I *really* have to fear from domestic entrapment? I was a single girl with a job living in a tenement apartment in the East Village in New York City with a posse of girlfriends who were like family. If I started knitting or even just vacuumed once in a while, the feminist police were not going to round me up.

So I started to dabble. Because my diet had consisted of cigarettes, coffee, and beer for far too long and my health had deteriorated to headaches and lethargy, I started with the obvious. I cut back on my beloved cigarettes and reduced the amount of alcohol to a few drinks a week. I read up on nutrition and started cooking for myself, reconnecting with my family heritage of good food. I made a commitment to running and practicing yoga.

Soon I felt better. And then a weird thing happened. As I took better care of my body, I grew unsatisfied with the lack of beauty in the rest of my life. Suddenly, after years of unkempt, uncared-for apartments, I wanted a nice home and lovely things in it. So I set out to create a real shelter.

Working on my apartment got me reinterested in crafts from those years in Girl Scouts: knitting, sewing, and cooking. I borrowed old home economics books from the library and read about hospital corners, proper dusting techniques, stain removal, and sewing basics. I even got secret subscriptions to *Martha Stewart Living* and *Gourmet*.

And you know what I learned? All the stuff that I had always dismissed as stupid women's work is actually quite complicated. There are systems and rules for doing it well—and they are not obvious, nor are they being taught in most school systems. Be honest: Do you know how to sew on a button or make curtains, let alone make dinner for eight without losing your mind? I sure didn't—and none of my friends did either. We were domestically challenged.

As I experimented with different tasks, I discovered which ones I liked (cooking, building shelves, decorating my apartment, and simple knitting), and which ones I hated (quilting, ironing, and dusting). I learned that my favorite thing to do in the whole world is to grocery shop—I love to be around food, to smell it, touch it, and think about all the delicious things I'm going to make in the kitchen.

I stopped fretting and embraced my inner craftiness. Yet, even with all this joyous creativity—and for me, domesticity is a very artistic process—there are times when I wonder: Am I too crafty, too girly? After all, our culture continues to thumb its nose at domesticity. When I make a meal for a couple of friends—something I have researched, read about, shopped for, and prepared—we enjoy it and then it's gone. It isn't important in the economic system—I don't make money from it, and it doesn't have the cultural capital of, say, writing a novel or making a sculpture.

More troubling for me is that it isn't just mainstream culture that dismisses domesticity, but some feminists as well. When Betty Friedan searched for the cause of "the problem that has no name" affecting middle-class white suburban housewives in 1963, she found it in housecleaning and caring for the family. According to Friedan, all things domestic were actually the root of women's malaise and depression. As I read through *The Feminine Mystique* now, forty years later, I have a lot of sympathy and admiration for Friedan as someone who was trying to make sense of her world. But I think her analysis is too narrow. It isn't the activity of housework that is so stifling, but rather that women had so few other options and, more important, that women's work has always been devalued.

From cooking to cleaning to caring for children, our culture views women's work as stupid, simple, suffocating—things that can easily be replaced by mechanization, crappy fast food, hiring poor women, and neglect—precisely because women have always done them. Even feminists aren't free from this type of thinking; we have internalized patriarchy to such an extent that we also dismiss our own history. And although we may not be aware of it, we have bought into the lie that women are inferior so we set out to be more like men: important, big, self-centered, and good at getting ours.

Debbie Stoller, the founder and editor of the third-wave feminist magazine *Bust,* believes that if women want to achieve complete equality, we have to honor domesticity. "We already know what's respectable and fulfilling about the workplace—basically going out and making money—and there is a certain amount of pride and independence in doing that." Debbie continues, "But I think we need to relearn what's valuable and fulfilling in the private sector. The home, children, crafts, and making things."

What if, instead of dismissing domesticity, we thought of it as an important part of women's culture? Don't get me wrong. I am not suggesting that every woman should enjoy knitting and cooking and embroidery. But I am suggesting that we give women's work its props as something valuable, interesting, and important, just as knowing how to build a house, keeping accounting records, or playing basketball is. Skill, love, and creativity go into creating a nice home, making things by hand, and raising children. It's not stupid and it's not easy; it's damn hard work that we need to respect. Moreover, it is our history, and dismissing it only doubles the injustice already done to women who didn't have any choice but to be domestic in the first place.

Paradoxically, when I learned to respect and embrace domesticity, I became reacquainted with my teenage anger, which had led me to feminism so many years ago. I found myself frustrated by the dismissive looks I received for knitting on the subway or the way people related to me for being so concerned with buying the right cheese or arranging a lovely vase of flowers. With this anger and frustration, I started a Web zine called getcrafty.com, devoted to radical craftiness—a feminist home economics site, if you will. The site covers arts and crafts, cooking, relationships, home decor, and finances. Out motto is "making art out of everyday life."

The site has blossomed into an inspiring community of women around the United States (and beyond) who share ideas about domesticity, feminism, politics, makeup, jobs, art, life, and their favorite TV shows. We have one thing in common: We are all crafty.

Being crafty means living consciously and refusing to be defined by narrow labels and categories. It's about embracing life as complicated and contradictory and, out of this chaos, constructing identities that are feminist and domestic, masculine and feminine, strong and weak. It's painting racing stripes down muscle cars and driving them in homemade skirts and high heel shoes. It's getting together to knit in cafés and building intimacy online. It's swapping clothing. It's about being both fashion-obsessed and simultaneously upset by sweatshop labor practices. It's about being well read and a fan of *Buffy the Vampire Slayer*. It's not about being quiet or demure, but it means always trying to be nice. It's about making things with your hands. And, most important, it's about living life artistically, regardless of whether or not you are an Artist with a capital A.

So here I am now at the ripe old age of thirty-three. I no longer live alone in a tenement but rather in a one-bedroom apartment in Greenwich Village with a husband, a dog, and a baby. My life is much more domestic and mundane, yet also more varied and interesting than I ever imagined it would be when I was a teenager in the suburbs of Southern California. I didn't grow up to be a famous feminist writer; instead I practice feminism in the way I live my life, the clothes I wear, the home I live in, the food I eat, the company I keep. It's not glamorous, but it is fulfilling. Ironically, my experience is the exact opposite of those women Betty Friedan wrote about in *The Feminine Mystique*. For me, embracing domesticity and women's work has freed me from a feeling that life is meaningless. Best of all, I now have simple ways to give myself and others the gift of living well.

Get Crafty is a manifesto for what I call the New Domesticity, a movement committed to recognizing, exalting, and most of all enjoying the culture that women have built for millennia. In these pages you'll find a lot of tips and ideas to help you domesticate, but only from the vantage point of creating a more meaningful life. In other words, you will not find chapters on creating the perfect *Architectural Digest* abode, keeping your floors so clean you can eat off them, or organizing your junk drawer, because I don't think that's what life is about. I'm more interested in the community we experience during a long dinner party or the nourishment we get from a home that feels warm and comforting. The point of life is to take advantage of all the joy and beauty that surrounds us—and to ensure that it's there for others to relish.

How to Use This Book

Throughout *Get Crafty* you will find journal exercises, collage ideas, and recipes. Being crafty is about doing: making stuff, enriching your life, thinking about things in a new way, and reaching out to others. I'm asking you to take a leap of faith and do things you may think are silly or uncool, like writing about your clothing style or taking a quiz about which craft is right for you. All I ask is that you try it. Do one exercise that seems dumb and see what happens. If you don't find it useful, just skip those sections of the book.

You also will find ideas for being active in your community under the heading "Craftivism." Betsy Greer, an activist living in Chapel Hill, North Carolina, introduced me to the concept of Craftivism: using crafts and crafting to make the world a better place. Every time you create something with your hands and then give it away, that's Craftivism. By doing something as simple as knitting scarves for the local women's shelter or making sandwiches for the homeless, we not only enrich others' lives, but we in turn feel less hopeless about the world. You can find the latest information on the Craftivism movement on Betsy Greer's Web site: http://www.Craftivism.com.

1

THE JOY OF DOING IT YOURSELF

Getting Crafty

To wrap a soft, chunky, hand-knit scarf around your neck, to cover yourself with a well-worn quilt, its patches of fabric lovingly stitched together, to slip on a simple hot-pink skirt that you sewed yourself is to know the power of crafts.

What's so satisfying about crafting? Maybe it has something to do with all the transformations that occur. When we craft, we make something from nothing. We take a pile of yarn and knit it into a sweater. We rip up old beauty magazines, repurposing the images, to create collages. Bananas, eggs, flour, and maple syrup become a sweet breakfast treat. To craft is to be in touch with the extraordinary aspects of life.

What I'm talking about is alchemy. The seemingly miraculous change of a thing into something better (thank you, *Webster's Dictionary*). Think about the last time you made bread from scratch.

> You are an alchemist;
> make gold of that.
>
> —WILLIAM
> SHAKESPEARE, *from*
> Timon of Athens

First there was flour, yeast, and water. You mixed them together, let that mixture rise, then you kneaded it, and baked it. A wonderful chemical reaction took place and you had something entirely new, bread. How amazing!

Part of the joy in crafting comes from knowing you made it. When you bake bread instead of buying it, you are not a passive consumer but a creator. You feel empowered. When you build a bookshelf rather than head over to Ikea, you actually know the idiosyncrasies of the wood. You know how many screws it took to make it sturdy. You get to choose the exact color of the stain. At the end of the process you say to yourself, "I made this!"

Doing it yourself is also relaxing. In fact, recent studies have shown that brain chemistry during knitting is similar to when doing yoga or meditating. This doesn't surprise me; I find the repetitive process of knitting soothing. Each stitch is like a mantra. And when I cook, I enter another dimension, a place of quiet enjoyment and sensual pleasure. Chopping, kneading, mixing, stirring are as calming to me as sitting in the lotus position and trying to empty my mind.

Plenty of women craft as a way to deal with the stress of their careers. Kari, a twenty-five-year-old environmental engineer from Tennessee, started knitting as a diversion from her often-demanding job. "In my line of work, projects can take twenty years to complete," says Kari. "This can be frustrating. Knitting, on the other hand, is a very methodical craft that has a clear beginning, middle, and end." Two years ago, when Kari's friend bought her wool and a few patterns, she was a bit nervous about whether she actually could knit. She always felt creative but had a hard time expressing herself. "I am no good at drawing," says Kari, "so I felt like I wasn't truly creative. But then I started knitting, which gave me the proof I needed."

Artistically, Kari feels that she tapped into a new side of herself. She says: "I've been working really hard for the last two years to stop identifying myself by my job. Now when people say to me 'So, what do you do?' I'm able to answer smoothly, 'Well, I read a

Made by hand, the craft object bears the fingerprints, real or metaphorical, of the person who fashioned it. These fingerprints are not the equivalent of the artist's signature, for they are not a name. Nor are they a mark or a brand. They are a sign: the almost invisible scar commemorating our original brotherhood or sisterhood.

—OCTAVIO PAZ, *from "Seeing and Using: Art and Craftsmanship"* lot, and I've been knitting this hat. . . .' It's really freeing to step out of your profession like that and to present yourself to others as a more rounded person."

Simply by learning to knit, Kari managed to change the way she sees herself. I initially met her on Glitter, the getcrafty.com message board, where we discussed the joys of knitting. When I finally met her in a bright, loftlike café in downtown New York City, she was a whirlwind of craftiness, wearing a funky business suit with Swedish Army leg warmers, red clogs, and a white wool hat that she had knit herself and then put in the drier for a felted effect. Whereas she once felt like a boring engineer, she has blossomed into an artistic force.

Kari recently has branched out into making her own clothing. "I hate shopping for new clothes," she says. "If I make them myself, I enjoy them much more and they fit better." By making clothes herself, Kari can custom tailor not only the size, but the fabric as well. She can create unique looks that no one else has.

Clearly, crafting has become a lifestyle choice. Criticism of shopping and consumerism often come up when speaking with people who identify with the New Domesticity. With the terrible working conditions in Third World factories, the anticonsumerist decision to craft is alluring. It becomes a political decision. Sandra, twenty-eight and living in Austin, Texas, is so committed to ending sweatshop practices that she now buys about 60 percent of her clothing from thrift stores and makes about 30 percent herself. The rest, things like underwear and socks, she tries to buy from companies that do not use child or sweatshop labor. Interestingly, although her entrée into crafts was through a political awakening, she learned to love sewing, which she hadn't expected. "I have always been a bit of a tomboy, neglecting my appearance and talking politics and drinking with the boys," claims Sandra. "But now that I have started sewing, I'm really loving crafts and rediscovering all these domestic things I never would have thought I'd like." Including a love of fashion and a mean quilting habit.

Lisa, a single mom living in Nyack, New York, started making her own soap in her basement because she didn't like the quality of grocery store brands and couldn't afford fancy soaps sold in specialty shops. "I wanted to wash my children with products that didn't have a lot of chemicals or harsh ingredients." So she made friends with some local farmers and started experimenting with different organic herbs and pure oils. "I researched the healing qualities of plants and other ingredients and found that I could create something really nice not only for my family but for friends as well." She soon started a little mail-order company called Brickhouse soap, selling to local stores and farmer's markets.

Not everyone has the time or inclination to devote to complicated endeavors, but that doesn't mean they aren't crafty. My best friend, Laura, would never commit to sewing all her own clothing or making her own soap. She works way too many hours and travels too often. Her craftiness comes out in the incredible meals she cooks for her friends. The last time I was over at her house we had a salad of tomatoes, crushed olives, and basil; roasted fennel and leeks topped with parmesan; and tilapia roasted in olive oil. Her menus are creative masterpieces, the table is always elegant but relaxed, the mood is open. Laura crafts not only because she enjoys it, but because it helps build community, something very dear to her.

To be honest, I craft out of pure selfishness. Although I love to make gifts for my friends and I appreciate that every time I craft something I am not consuming, mostly I create because it makes me feel good. When I feel anxious, I usually start up a scarf. (I like the simplicity of scarves.) When I'm stuck on an essay, I go into the kitchen and start cooking. In the process of cutting, chopping, and stirring, I can usually get past my writer's block. Despairing over a bad phone conversation, I make a collage and, in the course of cutting and pasting (not to mention swearing), I figure out how to make amends with my friend. I find the magic of crafts to be intensely personal and healing.

The great thing about the age we live in is that crafting is now a choice. We don't have to knit our sweaters or grow our own vegetables, which frees us up to do all sorts of other things. But the postindustrial era has also robbed us of all the benefits of crafting. The good news is that they are still here for your enjoyment. You can pick and choose. You can knit a scarf to go with your store-bought coat. You can cook your lunch and then eat dinner at a restaurant. You can tap into the joys of crafting without having to forsake all the wonderful modern amenities we have at our disposal.

The truth is, how you construct your creative time is up to you. There are all sorts of ways to get crafty. Whether it's cooking dinner, building a Web site, or just taking time out to place brightly colored stickers on your calendar, remember that you are an alchemist and that you have the ability to make something out of nothing.

> Whatever it is that pulls the pin, that hurls you past the boundaries of your own life into a brief and total beauty, even for a moment, it is enough.
>
> —JEANETTE WINTERSON, *from* Gut Symmetries

Which Craft Is Right for You?

Over the years I have tried many crafts, only to realize midway through some large project that I hated it. I have now settled on a few favorites: cooking, collaging, and knitting. It takes awhile to find the right craft; it's a very personal thing. That said, different skills are needed for different crafts, and knowing this before you invest in equipment and supplies is a good thing.

In general, I have found that less detail-oriented people enjoy cooking, which includes a lot of improvisation and creative flair. Baking is a more exact science and allows for fewer mistakes, something a perfectionist might cherish. Quilting can be very visual and artistic, but you need patience and perseverance. Sewing takes an exactitude and willingness to measure things, plus creativity and style to pull it all together. Knitting requires simple math, unless you're like me and just make scarves. Needlepoint is a low-investment craft, requiring only that you buy a kit and match up the colors. Gardening is for people who love nature and aren't afraid to get dirty. The following quiz will help you figure out which craft is right for you.

1. When reading a book you simply adore, you:
   a. Savor each page and read it slowly so it will last.
   b. Devour the entire book in one afternoon.

2. Did you make your bed this morning?
   a. Yes
   b. No

3. Does dirt under your fingernails send you running to the manicurist?
   a. Yes
   b. No

4. Are you now, or have you ever been, a smoker?
   a. Yes
   b. No

5. If you see a crooked painting hanging on a friend's wall, do you straighten it?
   a. Yes
   b. No

6. Do you like math?
   a. Yes
   b. No

7. Is your fridge covered in retro magnets and postcards?
   a. Yes
   b. No

8. Spotting a gorgeous basket of plump, bright-red juicy strawberries at the store, your first inclination is to:
   a. Pick them up and breathe in their fragrance.
   b. Admire the color and beauty.

	ATTENTION TO DETAILS	PATIENCE	WILLINGNESS TO GET DIRTY	VISUAL ACUITY	IMPROVISATION	CREATIVE FLAIR	MATH
KNIITING	X	X				X	X
SEWING	X	X		X		X	X
NEDDLECRAFTS (EMBROIDERY, NEEDLEPOINT, ETC.)		X		X		X	
QUILTING		X		X		X	
CUT-N-PASTE (DECOUPAGE, COLLAGE, SCRAPBOOKING)			X	X	X	X	
COOKING			X		X	X	
BAKING	X		X			X	X
GARDENING		X	X	X		X	

ANSWERS:

1. If you answered:
   a. Long-term projects like quilting and gardening might be nice for you.
   b. You might seek a more short-term craft like cooking, baking, and cut-n-paste crafts.

2. If you answered:
   a. You are most likely detail-oriented and might like knitting, needle-crafts, and sewing.
   b. You are possibly less detail-oriented, preferring gardening, cut-n-paste crafts, or cooking.

3. If you answered:
   a. You probably won't enjoy gardening, cooking, or baking; they can be quite messy.
   b. If you don't mind digging in the dirt, gardening could be your thing.

4. If you answered:
   a. Smokers and ex-smokers tend to love knitting. It gives us something to do with all of our nervous energy.
   b. Just remember: You don't have to be a smoker to be a knitter!

5. If you answered:

    a. You like things to be neat and ordered. Ever tried sewing?

    b. Maybe you don't care so much about silly details. Cooking may be your calling.

6. If you answered:

    a. Knitting often involves math. You could really shine at this craft.

    b. Fortunately, gardening requires no math whatsoever!

7. If you answered:

    a. Cut-n-paste crafts like decoupage will allow you to utilize all your vintage postcards and magazines.

    b. Maybe you should do something with what's inside your fridge? How about cooking?

8. If you answered:

    a. You are obviously quite sensual, and cooking or gardening might be just the thing.

    b. You are visually oriented and could enjoy sewing, quilting, needle-crafts, or cut-n-pasting.

Make Your Own Gifts

If you are new to crafts, making handmade gifts is a great place to start: They can be quite simple and instantly satisfying. You get the gratification of making it and your friends feel the love when they open it! Here are a few ideas to get you started.

DIY CARDS

A simple homemade card goes a long way to make a plate of cookies or a bouquet of flowers all the more meaningful. This recipe calls for images found in old magazines or from vintage postcards, but truly, all sorts of pictures can work here. Even pages torn from contemporary fashion magazines (abstract images of objects like flowers work best) or newspaper headlines (you can piece phrases together for new meanings) can be repurposed into interesting cards.

> 8½ x 11-inch colored card stock
>
> Scissors
>
> Images torn from old magazines or newspapers, vintage postcards, or photographs. All of these are easily found at garage sales, estate sales, and thrift shops. (For more information on finding things secondhand, see Chapter 3.)
>
> Elmer's glue or Modge Podge (can be purchased at craft supply stores)
>
> Small paintbrush

Cut a sheet of colored card stock in half width-wise. Fold one of the halves in half, creating a card. Arrange your image or images on the front of the card, then glue (or Modge Podge) them into place. Once they dry, using the paintbrush, brush glue or Modge Podge over the entire front of the card. This will create a decoupage effect. At first it will look white and yucky. Don't worry. Once it dries (about 10 to 15 minutes), it will provide a hard and stable finish. Experiment with the size of the card stock to create bookmarks, postcards, or name cards.

FLORA Y FAUNA SOAP

I developed this recipe back in the early 1990s when Laura and I started our own soap company. We called ourselves Flora Y Fauna and turned our shared apartment into a soap-making factory. When we weren't creating salt baths and herbal hangover remedies, we were drinking vast amounts of beer and dreaming about our millions.

Unfortunately, a few months into the venture, our entire inventory was stolen from Laura's car. Viewing the burglary as a sign, we left the soap business as quickly as we entered it. I look back on that time fondly, even though all I ended up with was debt and a kick-ass soap recipe.

What makes this soap recipe so appealing is that it doesn't require working with lye or other volatile ingredients. Instead, you simply grate pure coconut soap and melt it down with water, oil, and herbs to create beautiful, fancy-looking, good-smelling soaps.

This recipe yields 3 bars of soap.

2 bars Kirk's Coco Hardwater Castile. Do not try this with cheap imitation or brand-name soap. They will not melt down properly.

⅓ cup boiling water

¼ cup almond or olive oil, plus extra for greasing the molds

Additional herbs and essential oils to season your soap. Here are just a few suggestions:

- *Pretty Lady*: 2 tablespoons finely chopped dried rose petals and 6 drops rose essential oil
- *Relax, Don't Do It*: 2 tablespoons crushed lavender flowers and 8 drops lavender essential oil
- *Almond Delight*: 1 teaspoon vanilla extract, 3 tablespoons ground almonds (skin on), and 3 drops cinnamon oil
- *Wake Up, Little Susie*: 3 tablespoons finely chopped fresh rosemary and 6 drops eucalyptus oil
- *Clean-up Woman*: 10 drops tea tree oil

Box grater

Double boiler with lid (If you don't have a double boiler, you can create one by filling a large pot with 2 to 3 inches water and fitting a smaller heat-resistant pan or bowl on top of it. The sides of the pan can touch, but the bottoms must be separated by a few inches.)

Wooden spoon

Large bowl

Molds

Knife (optional)

Grate the soap.

Place grated soap in double boiler over medium heat and cover with a loose-fitting lid. Once water in double boiler begins to boil, add boiling water to soap, all at once. Mix slightly, then add almond or olive oil. Continue mixing until water is incorporated. The mixture should resemble mashed potatoes. Turn off heat.

Place soap mixture into large bowl. Add additional herbs and essential oils, and mix to incorporate fully.

Grease molds and hands with oil. Let the mixture cool slightly. Using your hands, scoop soap mixture out of bowl and press into molds. Use knife or index finger to smooth surface.

Store in a cool, airy place. It can take anywhere from 24 hours to 1 week for soap to harden, depending on the amount of liquid and optional ingredients you added, as well as the weather.

When soap is a nice firm texture (pressing into it with your finger doesn't leave an indent), cut around the edges and carefully ease it out of the mold. If you used a miniloaf pan, finish by slicing the soap into rectangle shapes with a kitchen knife. Store soap in waxed paper to maintain freshness.

LAURA'S LIMONCELLO

When my husband and I were in Bologna, Italy, on our honeymoon, we were given a shot of this lemony liqueur after dinner one night. Having already consumed a bottle of Prosecco, the local bubbly wine, we didn't want any more alcohol. But we didn't want to offend our friendly waiter, so we drank it anyway. The drink was deliciously refreshing: light and cool, sweet and tart, the perfect ending to a seafood meal on a warm July evening. We stumbled home, high from this city of great food and drink.

So when Laura presented me with a bottle of home-made limoncello this past Christmas, I was thrilled. The store-bought limoncello available in the United States is often cloyingly sweet and syrupy, nothing at all like what we had experienced in Bologna. This recipe creates a perfectly tart and lemony drink, just like they serve in Italy. Your friends will love it!

A small warning. Although this recipe could be made in a week, we recommend that you do it the old-fashioned way and take at least two months to let the alcohol infuse with the flavors of the lemon. There is so little in life that we have to wait for. Make a commitment to the full length of this recipe, and its flavor will be a sweet reward.

Makes approximately 12 cups of liquor, enough to fill three 750 ml wine bottles, with a little left over.

12 lemons (preferably organic)

6 cups of premium vodka (It's traditional to use Everclear alcohol, but Laura and I like Kettle One vodka best in this recipe.)

2½ cups sugar

2½ cups water

EQUIPMENT

Microplane or zester

Large glass or ceramic container with cover

1 ice cube tray

1 1-gallon plastic bag

Heavy saucepan

Wooden spoon

Mesh strainer

Funnel

> Glass bottles with tops (Laura bought lovely pink and red glass
>   bottles from Mexico for her batch. I used recycled wine
>   bottles and made my own labels.)

Using a microplane or zester, zest the rinds from 12 lemons, making sure to avoid the white part of the lemon peel.

Combine zest and 6 cups vodka into a large glass or ceramic container, cover, and store in a cool dark place for one month.

In the meantime, squeeze enough lemon juice to fill the ice cube tray. Once frozen, transfer the cubes to a plastic bag and keep frozen.

After allowing the vodka mixture to sit for one month, use a mesh strainer to remove the zest from the vodka, and discard.

Make simple syrup by heating sugar and water in heavy saucepan, stirring until sugar dissolves. Take care to not overheat, or it will turn into caramel.

Incorporate simple syrup into the "marinated" vodka, adding it in stages and tasting as you go along. The advantage of homemade limoncello over commercial brands is that you can control the sweetness.

Balance the blend's sweetness by adding lemon juice cubes to taste, stirring until melted.

Using the funnel, pour the mixture into your bottles. Cover and store once again in a cool dark place. The ideal time for the mixture to set is one month (or perhaps longer), but we've had decent results after just one week.

ALERT LIP GLOSS

Here's the scenario: You're in a long, boring meeting at work and about to fall asleep. Instead of reaching for another cup of coffee, reach for this lip gloss to refresh your senses instead! Made with peppermint essential oil, it's an easy (and cheap) gift that only takes a few minutes.

2 tablespoons petroleum jelly

¼ teaspoon lipstick (any color!)

8 drops peppermint essential oil

Put the petroleum jelly and the lipstick in a small microwave container. Microwave on high for 30 seconds or until the mixture has softened. (If you do not have a microwave, you can melt the jelly and lipstick together in an improvised double boiler: Fill a small pan with water and fit a smaller heat-resistant pan or bowl on top of it. The sides of the two pans may touch, but make sure that the bottom of the two pans are separated by a layer of water. Heat the lip gloss mixture in the double boiler until it has softened, about two minutes.)

Once ingredients have softened, blend well. Mix in peppermint oil. Place the gloss in a small container. Sealed, gloss will keep indefinitely.

OTHER GIFT IDEAS:

- Hand out a DIY card good for one homemade meal.
- Give the gift of housecleaning. Offer to spend the day spring-cleaning with a friend.
- Make a mixed tape or burn a mixed CD.
- Make a scrapbook of mementos and photos of time spent with your friend.

Cool Crafts

As more and more young women embrace the domestic arts, funky crafts emerge. The following are designed to show you that crafting doesn't have to be staid or boring. With a little creativity, you can create beautiful, kitsch, or ironic crafts for your home, wardrobe, or friends.

MAKE AN A-LINE SKIRT: IT'S SEW SIMPLE

This sewing project was contributed by Susan Beal, a crafty lady from Portland, Oregon, who organizes a local stitch-n-bitch (knitting group) and sells homemade skirts, bags, and jewelry on her Web site: http// www.susanstars.com.

I love this skirt because you can make it in one evening. Instead of following a pattern, you use an A-line skirt you already own as a guide. A word of advice: Don't get impatient and skip the ironing portion of the directions. Having your fabric well pressed is the key to good sewing.

Material. Choose a fabric that is a bit elastic. (Cotton requires a zipper, which is tricky.) Try a stretchy denim, glittery black, or nubby textured fabric. For a medium-size knee-length skirt (32-inch waist and 24 inches long), you'll need a piece of fabric at least 54 inches wide and about 30 inches long.

A-line skirt that fits you well

Tailor's chalk (You can find this at the fabric store. In a pinch, standard white chalk will do.)

Good scissors

Pins

Sewing machine with a 90/14 needle (Ball point or stretch needles are best.)

⅜-inch elastic (about 1 yard)

Cotton thread in the same or complementary color

Iron

Measuring tape

Elastic guide (available at sewing stores) or large safety pin

Fold your material in half, with the finished (selvage) edges of the pieces together, wrong side out. Place your skirt (the one that fits you perfectly) down on top of the fabric, flat and face up, so that one side is closest to the selvage edge and one side is closest to the fold.

Using your chalk, draw around the outline of the skirt, leaving an extra ½ to 1 inch of material on the sides and an extra 1½ to 2 inches on the top and bottom. (This extra material will become the waistband, hem, and sides of your new skirt.) Remove the skirt, then cut along the chalk line. You will end up with two trapezoid-shaped pieces.

After you've cut out the two pieces, fold them down the middle to check the sides, top, and bottom for symmetry. This doesn't have to be extremely precise, but it's better to leave too much than too little. (You can always tweak and narrow a skirt that's too big, but it's difficult to add fabric when the skirt is too tight or too short.) Check to see that the flare will be roughly equivalent on each side.

Lay the two pieces of fabric one on top of the other, right sides together. Pin one side together all the way down from top to bottom, about one pin every 3 to 4 inches. Then pin the other side the same way.

Now it's time to sit at your sewing machine. Put the stitch length on 6 or 8—it helps to have the stitches big, so they'll stretch with the material.

Stitch one side of the skirt from top to bottom, ⅝ inch from the edge. (Your sewing machine will have a guideline at ⅝ inches, so it's easy to follow.) Backstitch at the top and bottom of each side to hold the seam. Do the other side the same way.

Iron the two side seams open on the inside, so the extra material is lying flat.

To start the waistband, fold over about ½ inch of material from the top all the way around. Iron it flat as you go. Then fold over once again from the top ½ inch so there's a double thickness. Iron it flat again and pin it together every few inches.

Back to the sewing machine. Starting at the side seam, stitch close to the bottom edge of the waistband all the way around, stopping an inch or two before the side seam so there's enough room to feed the elastic into the waistband.

Thread the elastic through with a guide or large safety pin, and slide it into the waistband with your fingers pushing from the outside. Guide it all the way around the waistband. When the elastic comes out the other side, pull it as tight as you desire (usually so it puckers just a little bit evenly all the way around). Pin the elastic together and try on the skirt to ensure the waist feels comfortable.

Once you have found a comfortable fit, sew the two ends of the elastic together securely, either by hand or with the machine, making sure the elastic lies flat and doesn't twist. Then sew the last inch of the waistband close, backstitching to hold the seam.

Prep the hem the same way as the waistband: Fold over about ½ inch of material from the bottom all the way around, ironing it flat as you go. Then fold over once again from the bottom ½ inch so there's a double thickness. Iron it flat again and pin it together every few inches. I recommend finishing the skirt by hand-sewing the hem (which leaves no noticeable thread on the exterior of the skirt), but you also could finish it on the machine, using the same stitch as you did with the waistband.

Finish up by ironing your skirt one more time. That's it: a homemade skirt in just a few hours.

KNIT A BIKINI: STRING THEORY

Amanda Ray created this great bikini pattern for Bust *magazine. I love it so much, I begged them to let me reprint it here. (Note: My friend Tobi Armstrong and I made a few changes to simplify it.) This pattern is for intermediate to advanced knitters. Do not attempt this as your first project.*

Directions are for a medium bikini. (See instructions for making the pattern bigger.) It uses the stockinette stitch, a popular stitch that alternates a row of knitting with one of purling.

Gauge: 5 stitches = 1 inch/6 rows = 1 inch. Make sure to test your gauge by making a small swatch using your yarn and needles; if you're getting more than 5 stitches to the inch, try again using larger needles; if you're getting fewer than 5 stitches, try using smaller ones.

MATERIALS

3 skeins Cotton Classic by Tahki Imports (Note: When using skeins of yarn, always wind them into balls before you begin knitting. You've seen this done before; it's when one person holds the yarn up between two hands and the other person winds. In the absence of another person, you can use your own feet to hold the yarn.)

1 pair size 6 knitting needles (metal needles work best with cotton yarn)

1 size 1 crochet hook

1 yard elastic to match yarn color, or invisible (clear) elastic

Darning needle

BIKINI BOTTOM

Front: Cast on 62 stitches (or 66 for larger bottoms). Work in stockinette stitch for 14 rows, beginning with a purl row. (Work 20 rows for more coverage.) On row 14 (20), bind off 7 (or 9) stitches at beginning of row, continue knitting until only 7 (9) stitches remain on needle, then bind off these remaining stitches. Break yarn. Reattach yarn and purl your way back across the 48 stitches you have left on your needle. This is where you'll begin your descent to the crotch, so fasten your seat belt. This pattern is all about decreasing to make it easier, because increasing is a pain in the butt, trust me! Remember, you only decrease on knit rows. It's going to seem wacky, but in the end it will work.

First of all, to decrease, you will knit 2 stitches together. For decreases on edges like we're doing here, always do the decreases at least 2 stitches in from the end so that you make nice edges. Decrease 2 stitches at both sides of the bikini every other row for 16 rows until you have only 16 stitches left. (On every other row: knit 2, knit 2 together, knit 2 together again, then knit across the row until you have 6 stitches left on the needle. Then knit 2 together, knit 2 together again, and knit 2. You've decreased by 4 stitches.) Okay, now you're at the crotch. Without decreasing, continue knitting in stockinette stitch for 20 more rows, and bind off.

Back: Cast on 86 (90) stitches. Work in stockinette stitch for 14 rows (or 20, for more room in the seat). Just as you did on the front, on the 14th row (or 20th row), cast off 7 (9) stitches at the beginning and end of the row. Reattach the yarn and purl your way back. Decrease by 2 stitches on each side of the next, and every other row, for 28 rows, until you have only 16 stitches left. Work in stockinette stitch for 13 more rows. Bind off.

BIKINI TOP

Divide remaining yarn into 2 balls. We're going to make both triangles at once.

Directions are for a full-coverage A, a comfortable B, or a scanty C cup. If you decide you want more coverage or have a larger bust, just cast on 5 to 10 more stitches. The instructions will still work.

Cast on 33 stitches for each triangle. Work in stockinette stitch for 18 rows, then start decreasing 2 stitches on each side of every other row for 16 rows, until you have nothing left. Bind off, and you've got your tops!

All right, now you're really almost done. Take your crochet hook and make two 2-foot chains. Attach one to the top of each triangle. You can hand-sew these on. Now chain a third chain that's 4½ feet long. This is going to tie around your chest at the bottoms of the triangles. Attach the chain and the elastic to the triangles by using your knitting yarn and a darning needle. Use a whip stitch through the triangle, around the elastic, and then through the chain. When you are finished, sew one end of the elastic in place, adjust the tightness of the elastic, and sew the other end in place. Attach the chain to the triangles by making a single chain with your crochet hook along the bottoms of your triangles and around the long chain.

Assembly: Sew the crotch and sides together. You can hand-sew it using the darning needle and your knitting yarn, or you can use a sewing machine. (I used a sewing machine on mine.) Don't try it on yet, or you'll hate me.

Attach the elastic to the waist of the suit using the same method you did for the top, minus the chain. Single crochet over the elastic and around the waist of the suit, starting at a side seam. Now you can try it on. Pull the elastic to fit your waist and hug your butt. Sew the elastic together, smooth it out, and you're done.

VINYL FLOWER POTS: THE SOLUTION FOR OLD RECORDS

My friend Sandy Ryan developed this great use for old records. She melts them down in the oven and turns them into flowerpots!

12-inch records

1 oven-safe bowl, approximately 10 inches across the top and
  4½ inches across the base for standard-size albums

1 cookie sheet

The first and most important step is choosing which records to melt. Sandy advises shopping at the thrift stores or garage sales and melting someone else's memories, rather than destroying your own collection. But I say, if old albums are cluttering your home, melt 'em, baby!

Preheat oven to 200°.

Place the oven-safe bowl on the cookie sheet, top side down. Then place the record on top of the bowl.

Bake for 5 minutes.

Your record should now be flexible but not too hot to handle. Check this with a quick touch of your fingertip. The bowl and cookie sheet will get hotter than the record so make sure you use a potholder when moving them. Pull the record off the bowl, then quickly flip the bowl over and push the record down into it. Manipulate the sides to get it the shape you want.

Let cool. If record is not the desired shape, place it back in the oven and reheat.

Once completely cooled, you can add your favorite plant or flower! The record has a natural drain—the hole for sticking it on the turntable.

Freestyle Knitting

Tobi Armstrong is the master of knitting without a pattern. After choosing unique yarns, he creates scarves, shawls, and sweaters by eyeing things out and trial and error. If you are interested in knitting in this freestyle manner, here are a few of his suggestions.

- *You have to learn the rules before you can break them.* Learn the basics of knitting before you try doing it freestyle. Make lots of scarves, knit from patterns, and learn how things are constructed. For example, I went through a "sock" phase. For about a year and a half I felt compelled to hand-knit socks. Turning a sock heel is actually rather complicated. In the beginning I followed a pattern religiously. It took me several pairs before I was ready to start experimenting. Once I had the mechanics of the heel down, I was able to improvise. I started substituting big chunky yarns for the expected finer ones, modifying them to make lace-up booties and all kinds of wacky stuff. No matter how much I strayed from the pattern, the mechanics remained the same.

- *Look at everything like a ball of yarn.* I really like to knit with unexpected materials. Anything that is even vaguely a textile is fair game. Some of my most successful knitting projects weren't made with yarn. I once made a sweater with nylon twine from the hardware store. I made a shawl for a friend with vintage seam binding tape. I made a net bag out of bathing suit elastic.

- *Be prepared to screw up.* I have watched a number people embark on knitting projects in the following fashion: (1) They find a picture of a knitted thing in a magazine that they are crazy about; (2) they buy a bunch of really expensive yarn to make it with; (3) they start wildly knitting; (4) then, when it doesn't work, they get really bummed out and disappointed and hide the whole mess under the bed. You have to experiment and be prepared for your first attempts not to work. If something is not working, just pull it apart and start over. The joy of knitting is as much about the process as it is about the finished garment.

- *Make your projects a "melting pot."* Some of the coolest stuff I've made incorporates other crafting skills. The baby blanket I recently finished is a combo of quilting and knitting. I quilted squares of beautiful fabric and joined them all together with strips of knitted lace. I had a pattern for the lace strips (designing lace patterns is not for the faint of heart), but I did the rest of it by the seat of my pants. The finished piece is beautiful, and one of the things I love the most about it is the combination of the quilting and knitting.

- *Let it evolve.* When you are inventing things as you go along, they need room to change as they grow. Many of my projects have started as one thing and ended up something else entirely. I once made a sweater with a deeply plunging neckline for someone. When I was fitting it on her, we decided that it looked better backward—as a sexy backless number—and so that's how I finished it. Sometimes I find yarn or other material, buy it, and then it sits in a box for what seems like forever. Inevitably, one day I figure out what I'm supposed to do with it. Sometimes I'll stumble on materials to add to projects halfway through the process—beads or buttons or something—and I find room for them too. It's nice to let your knitting surprise you.

CRAFTIVISM

Crafty things you can do to make the world a little better:

- Buy yarn and knitting supplies from A Stitch in Time, an organization that helps at-risk teens learn vocational skills through running a knitting shop. Check out their Web site: http://www.astitchintime.bizhosting.com.
- Knit for homeless families. Warming Families provides clean blankets and clothing for those in need. They are looking for volunteers to knit or crochet blankets, hats, scarves, and mittens. They even provide patterns on their Web site: http://www.warmingfamilies.org.
- Make blankets for babies. Project Linus has over fifty chapters in the United States alone, this is a well-organized volunteer organization. Their Web site lists contact information for all chapters, along with details on how to start your own: http://www.projectlinus.org.
- For more organizations that accept handmade articles for charitable uses, check out Sewing Charity:
  http://www.dotdigital.com/sewingcharity.
- Help change manufacturing practices. Not all of us can afford the time or the money to make our clothing. Sometimes we find ourselves shopping at large retailers with exploitive factories located in the Third World. Don't despair! There are still things you can do as a consumer to change these conditions. For more information, check out:
  http://www.sweatshops.org.

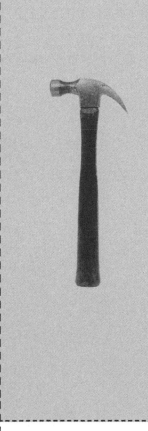

Links

ONLINE KNITTING

Although my grandmother Meme initially taught me how to knit, I forgot how to cast-off before I was finished with my first scarf. Desperate to finish it one night at 2:00 A.M., I went online looking for instructions and discovered About.com's great knitting site. Not only do they feature excellent, simple instructions, they offer free patterns. This is the perfect site for the beginning knitter. http://knitting.about.com/bllearn.htm.

CRAFTY E-ZINES

KNITTY: PURLS OF WISDOM

Super-cute Web site devoted to knitters. Patterns include color photos, and articles cover all sorts of crafty topics including knitting away the baby blues and copyrighting your patterns. http://www.knitty.com/ISSUEfall03/index.html.

NOT MARTHA

Megan Reardon is not Ms. Stewart, but she's definitely crafty. Her site offers advice on making cotton man-scarves and a skirt out of a pair of jeans, among other equally edgy projects. http://www.megan.scatterbrain.org/notmartha/tomake/jeanskirt.html.

SUBLIME STITCHING

The hippest embroidery site ever. Jenny Hart sells patterns and kits to warm a crafty lady's heart: White Stripes postcards, "Feed Me" baby bibs, and martini hand towels are just a few of her offerings. http://www.sublimestitching.com/index.html.

Resources

A FEW GOOD BOOKS

Once you have decided to dive into a new craft project, do a little research. This will help you figure out the right tools and equipment, as well as give you the basic information to get started. Check out your local library for how-to books, which will offer patterns and instruction. Unfortunately, the photography and designs of many of these books are often outdated and dull, but that's where your imagination comes in! Here are a few books that I recommend.

Reader's Digest Complete Guide to Sewing
Although I'm not crazy about all the patterns, this book is a good place to start for the beginner sewer.

Encyclopedia of Craft Projects for the First Timer by Ann Benson, Vanessa-Ann, and Linda Orton
Unfortunately, I have not been able to find any great books on scrapbooking, candle-making, and beading. The photography and examples in this craft overview are a bit square, but if you can look past the style, the instructions are clear.

Encyclopedia of Embroidery Techniques by Pauline Brown
This comprehensive book not only covers every stitch and technique but also explores the history of embroidery and its traditional uses.

Fabric Savvy: The Essential Guide for Every Sewer by Sandra Betzina et al.
A very good overview of fabrics.

The Good Housekeeping Illustrated Book of Needlecrafts
A standard book on needlecrafts. Good for beginners.

How to Grow Fresh Air: 50 Houseplants That Purify Your Home or Office by B. C. Wolverton

This is a great book for gardening types who want to learn more about healing plants.

The Knit Stitch: The Knitting Experience by Sally Melville

Sally Melville introduces knitting to the novice, giving excellent instructions as well as a ton of color photos that explain everything.

Knitting in Plain English by Maggie Righetti

A great beginner book, with helpful advice for not only starting projects but correcting mistakes as you go.

La Casa Loca: Latino Style Comes Home 45 Funky Craft Projects for Decorating & Entertaining by Kathy Cano-Murillo

Kathy Cano-Murillo is a crafty lady from Phoenix. Her book features incredibly creative and cool craft projects, like how to turn a soft-drink bottle into a fabulous Glitter-y vase. I highly recommend this book.

The Quilts of Gee's Bend by John Beardsley

This book features quilts from Gee's Bend, an isolated area of Alabama with a tiny population of former slaves who, over the past hundred or so years, have developed a unique quilting style. Although the book is not a how-to, the photographs of these highly creative, abstract quilts are thoroughly inspirational.

Circles of the East: Quilt Designs from Ancient Japanese Family Crests by Kumiko Sudo

Beautiful Japanese designs with how-to instructions.

Stitch-n-Bitch: The Knitter's Handbook by Debbie Stoller

This is a hip knitting book from the editor of *Bust* magazine. It offers good instructions and, better yet, cool patterns. If you buy only one knitting book, this is the one.

2 THE IMPORTANCE OF HOME

Gimme Shelter

After years of living in a dark, ugly tenement apartment in Manhattan's East Village, with the requisite futon on the floor, piles of dirty clothing thrown in the corner, and very little else, I decided I wanted a *real* home. This nesting instinct took me by surprise; I had never been a real homebody. I hated cleaning and had been perfectly willing to live out of my suitcase. Recently, though, I had started to dread returning to the mess that was my apartment and to feel jealous of friends who had warm, comfortable, inviting spaces. And so, with very little decorating knowledge, I decided to "remodel" my 350-square-foot abode.

I began my fix-it journey one freezing February day by hitting the home decoration section of the local mega-bookstore. I grew dizzy and faint and my eyes glazed over as I surveyed hundreds of

Home is a name, a word, it is a strong one; stronger than magician ever spoke, or spirit ever answered to, in the strongest conjuration.

—CHARLES DICKENS, *from* Martin Chuzzlewit

glossy books, from how-to guides for the apparent idiot, to hints for the well heeled and flush with cash. The cool contingent was represented by globe-trotting hipsters in mod clothing surrounded by 1960s-inspired designs. The standards were present as well: the conservative magazine brands from an older generation, repurposed and reshot for today's market. There were books devoted to Japanese decor, with rock fountains, black marble countertops, red doors, and petite oatmeal-colored vases. Several books addressed the flat-roof, midcentury modern approach. These homes were built in places like Palm Springs and filled with abstract art and Danish modern furniture: all clean lines and sensual curves, whispering toward a future that never happened. There were volumes on Mexican adobes, standing squat and white against a wide Sante Fe sky, in which brick-colored tiles met arched hallways and white fireplaces and antique couches covered with Native American quilts filled living rooms. Then there were books devoted to the new McMansions, with their plush green carpets, yellow wallpaper, and prodigious use of floral upholstery. As I flipped through the pages of each book, I grew more and more alarmed. Was I beyond help? I was too poor to be a new-design hipster, too hip for the suburban flowers-on-steroids treatment, and too smart to take advice from a "dummy" book. I needed help creating a shelter, but none of these books felt right.

Feeling discouraged, I went home, closed my eyes, and started to imagine what I wanted my apartment to look like. The answers came slowly. First, I had to be realistic about my finances. Given that I was in serious credit card debt, I would have to be creative in my approach. I got a library card and took out a few home economic and interior design books, merely for suggestions. I gleaned slick decorating magazines from my neighbors' recycling piles and flipped through the pages, clipping any images that appealed: rooms crowded with antiques, birds in flight, bright green apples, cups full of coffee with milk, purple flower arrangements, and a photograph of sunlight hitting a tree with its leaves various shades of burnt orange, yellow, and red. I placed these in a file while I searched for more, learning what I liked as I went. After about a month of doing this, I made a collage with all these mismatched images, refusing to place anything into a category or style. And then I started plotting.

I painted the walls in complementary colors: a yellow green for the "kitchen" (it was more of a closet with an oven and a sink), various shades of café con leche for the living room, and a lovely pale blue for the bedroom. I found painting boring and difficult, but also oddly therapeutic; it cleared my head and kept me focused. I bought a real mattress and box spring and cajoled a friend to build a high platform for it (I used the lower portion for storage) and added bookshelves to the bedroom. At a thrift store, I found a painting of a woman sitting in a sunny corner writing a letter, as well as a few portraits of flower arrangements. I hung cream-colored linen curtains and got a sisal rug for the living room. I even managed to fit a small white table with yellow chairs from the flea market into a taxicab and got neighbors to help me bring them up the stairs.

I finally had furniture and a real bed, but something still wasn't right. My friend Cabiria has this great saying about life—"It's no use trying to buy oranges at the hardware store"—and it was dawning on me that this maxim needed to be applied to my home. The fake wood cabinets in the "kitchen" just didn't work. After hours of scrubbing, the floors were no longer a filthy dishwater gray, but they were still linoleum. And my apartment was still very, very dark, so dark that I had to keep the lights on during the day, the kind of dark that gives you an excuse to sleep in and stay up late. After a year of slow progress on my decorating plan, it was clear that what I longed for was sunlight, and this apartment had none.

I moved. With enough pestering, I convinced my landlord to rent me the vacant apartment on the sixth floor of my building, even though there was no elevator. The walk up those five flights

You play, you win, you play, you lose. You play. It's the playing that's irresistible. Diving from one year to the next with the things you love, what you risk reveals what you value.

—JEANETTE WINTERSON, *from* The Passion

of stairs was exhausting, even without groceries. Who cares? I thought. At least I have sunlight, a view, and an eat-in kitchen!

The day I moved, I knew I got it; the new space was, as Goldilocks would say, "just right." I found an *I Love Lucy* gold couch with clean lines in excellent condition at a secondhand store in the outer boroughs. It fit perfectly in the corner. I got rid of my TV, so that the couch became a wonderful space to read books, dream, and drink champagne with a dear girlfriend or two. I kept the walls white, threw out the sisal rug, and left the floors to the bare gray carpet. I found two bookshelves on the street: one to hold my cookbooks in my eat-in kitchen and the other to house the collection of books I have been schlepping around with me since college. I hung my paintings in the living room. The bedroom was so tiny it fit only my bed and some clothes. I kept it simple.

Something was still missing. I had been writing at my kitchen table, but what I yearned for was a real desk. One day I got a call from a friend. He had found a beautiful old oak door that had once graced the New York City high school where Tony Bennett and the Rosenbergs had gone. The door was about ten feet high and four feet wide; did I want it? Absolutely! I cut the door down and used the scraps to build legs, turning it into a large, long table that took over most of my living room. It was a pleasure to spend evenings and weekends sitting there, typing on my laptop computer. I did a lot more writing than I had ever done.

I loved that apartment. The funny thing is that it wasn't special by anyone else's standards. It would never have been featured in a magazine spread; it didn't hold any designer furniture and it wasn't immaculate. But for me, it was perfect.

As I'm writing this now, I'm looking out large windows onto a cold snowy New York in the apartment I now share with my husband. (I fell madly in love with, then married, the guy who found the door on the street.) I have a new desk; the old monster wouldn't fit in our living room. My books surround me. A sign with the quotation "Do not fear the mistakes, there are none" from Miles Davis keeps me going when I feel scared and doubtful. I have drawers of collage material, arts and crafts supplies, knitting needles and wool. There is a statue of a smirking Buddha to my left. He reminds me to take it slow. A CD compilation of surf music is playing in the background. My home is the creative, sunny shelter I always dreamed about.

Creating Your Space

The biggest lesson I learned during my three-year search for shelter is that you don't have to follow some preordained set of rules. Case in point: In my current apartment, the robin's-egg-blue living room walls clash perfectly with our vintage Cabernet Sauvignon–colored velvet couch. We have Turkish and Oriental rugs on the floors, a gigantic dark oak dining room table in the corner, plus two palm trees and bamboo window coverings. The bright pink bedroom walls are lined with bookshelves that we made ourselves out of cheap pine stained deep brown and varnished. They hold my husband's thousand-plus books. On the walls, we chose antique drawings of New York and Paris, two of our favorite cities. The hallway features a portrait of our dog in which he stands proudly against a backdrop of tumultuous pink sky. Over the years we've acquired artwork from friends and family, none of which matches any other in style or substance, but all bring us great joy.

As someone whose own home decor can be summed up by "Dumpster diver meets French colonial," I encourage you to make your space exactly as you like it. Consider three of my friends and their approaches to decorating. First there is Kate, a thirty-four-year-old independent filmmaker living in Brooklyn, on a very small income. I like to call her style American eccentric. Her two-bedroom apartment is chock full of beautiful, odd, and sometimes ironic finds from thrift stores across the country. Her bathroom is stuffed with paintings of Che Guevara and dogs smoking cigars.

Too much attention to the looks of the home can backfire if it creates a stage-set feeling instead of the authenticity of a genuinely homey place.

—CHERYL MENDELSON, *from* Home Comforts

The paw and tail of a Chinese porcelain tiger balance a large piece of glass creating a coffee table in her living room; in the kitchen is a purple couch. She invested in a few beautiful large rugs for her hardwood floors and then, to line the windows, found potted trees that someone had left in the trash. An old quilted spread covers the bed. Her home is cluttered and homey and filled with cats, and the subway rattles her windows as it runs by. As someone who writes and works at home, Kate has created a whimsical space that nurtures her.

In contrast is Laura, who lives in Lower Manhattan and is the creative director of marketing for a travel magazine. She likes to knit on planes, which means she gets a lot of knitting done, as she spends a third of her time flying around the world. Her apartment is a testimony to both her travels and her philosophy of home as sanctuary. There is no clutter in her minimalist one bedroom (and she says she doesn't relate to being a Virgo!). The living room is centered around a Moroccan door that she transformed into a very low table. Surrounding it are purple and green pillows, which cushion her friends' bottoms during her famous dinner parties. Her kitchen shelves are open and lined with fine olive oils, exotic liqueurs, tea, and imported dried pastas. The feeling of her space is spare, serene, and comforting. It's a peaceful respite from her fast-paced life.

Finally, we have Barbara, who is a nurse in Portland, Oregon. Barbara has no patience for antiquing or thrifting. She'd rather read a book or take a hike than go searching for the perfect end table. The two-bedroom house that she shares with her girlfriend is full of new furniture but still feels personal. Her choice of soothing avocado-green paint in the bedroom makes the simple store-bought bed and dressers warm and inviting. By introducing framed album cover posters in the living room, the plain couch and coffee table don't seem so generic. The white shelves are lined with books. A simple wicker chair in the corner with a nice lamp and small table create the perfect reading nook. Her house makes you think of afternoons spent sipping chamomile tea and eating banana bread.

By being honest with what she wants to spend her time on, Barbara was able to create a home with all-new, low-priced furniture that still manages to feel authentic.

The lesson? It's not what your house looks like that matters. What matters is how you feel when you're in it. The argument I make, and make loudly, is that your home should be a thoughtful testament to what you need. Living in an unhappy, undecorated space will affect how you feel about yourself and the world. Whether you slap on some paint, pull in some furniture off the street, or rent a truck and head out to a furniture emporium, you will be surprised at what the right space can do for your state of mind.

You start and end your days at home. It's where you let your defenses down. It's the place where you eat, watch *Breakfast at Tiffany's*, talk on the phone, get ready for dates, raise children, cook dinner, and entertain. And for many of us, it's also the place where we work, either part or full time. Given how important this space is, don't let your home just happen. Self-consciously create something that can nourish you; it will help the rest of your life.

Things a Home Should Provide

A few things you should think about as you prepare to decorate:

- *Security.* It's important to feel safe. Make sure you have sturdy locks and secured windows.
- *Creativity.* Your home should inspire you. Paint walls favorite colors, clip striking images and hang them near your desk, buy art, and fill your home with incredible music. Have people over who are stimulating.
- *Reprieve.* The world is hard. The air is polluted. The roads are hectic. The grocery lines are long. Our jobs are competitive

and tiring. The home has the potential to offer a respite from the craziness of the world, not to avoid reality but as a place to recharge.

- *Comfort in times of sickness.* There is nothing worse than being sick in a dirty, empty apartment that lacks amenities. Be prepared. Keep ibuprofen and cold medicine stocked. Frozen or canned chicken broth can be heated in a pinch. Good books and a few DVDs can make recovery much more enjoyable. The next time you get sick, make a list of things that would soothe you. When you recover, make it a priority to buy them.

- *Romance.* The possibilities are endless: Light candles and enjoy a glass of wine for one, serve your family a picnic of fried chicken and coleslaw right on the living room floor, draw a bubble bath for you and your lover, or give the baby growing in your stomach a little massage with lavender oil. Doing romantic things will create a romantic home.

- *Active enjoyment.* Whether it's cooking, writing, quilting, painting, or playing with your cats, nurture some hobby or art other than watching television. Having supplies and material to do your favorite things makes your home a fun, active place. Once you put away what my friend Kate calls "Satan" (aka TV), you will learn to equate your home with happy activity rather than passivity.

CUT-N-PASTE: THE HOME COLLAGE

Art therapists have been using collages for decades to help patients process their emotions. I find them useful as a tool to explore desire and taste. Images help us go beyond language to express what it is we are looking for. The very act of searching for things we like opens us up to new ideas. Plus, who doesn't like cutting and pasting? The second part of this exercise is to do a little journaling. Once you've freed up the imagination through collaging, putting words to paper is a way to go even further. I've listed questions to help you get the ball rolling, but free writing is just as effective.

> 10 (or more) magazines (rather than purchasing them, you may want to check the curbs in your neighborhood on recycling day.)
> Scissors
> Glue sticks or multipurpose glue
> One large poster board
> Journal and pen

Set aside an hour for this exercise.

First, create a mood. Light incense, play music, open a bottle of wine, or whatever suits you. Unplug the phone and tell your roommates or loved ones not to disturb you.

Next, go through the magazines and tear out images that reflect qualities you want in your home. Don't be practical! This is your time to be frivolous and extravagant. The collage is not meant to be literal, but rather to help you visualize your desires. For example, my friend Emma, an ex–Los Angeleno living in Paris, has a lot of images of water in her Home Collage. This doesn't mean she needs to buy a house with a pool or move to Malibu, but she might use this as inspiration to paint her bathroom blue and add framed images from surfing magazines to the walls. The point of this exercise is to relax and play with your home decor, without the weight of doing it "right."

Once you've collected twenty to thirty images, arrange them and glue them on to your poster board, in whatever manner seems right. Then take some time to look at it and write about what you see in your journal.

1. What are some of the similarities in your images?
2. What kinds of things are you drawn to?
3. List five qualities from your collage that you'd like your home to have.
4. List two things you can do this week to make this a reality.

Ten Tips for Easy Home Improvement

1. *Paint.* Even white paint can freshen up a home. You will be amazed at what this simple thing will do to improve your space.

2. *Rearrange the furniture.* By making her living room the bedroom and the bedroom the living room, my friend Gayle found that she didn't need to move after all. Try your favorite chair in a new place near the window. Play with having your desk in the dining room. The worst thing that can happen is that you have to move it all back.

3. *Buy plants.* Plants can make any space feel homey. Try big old bamboo palms. Not only are they very hard to kill and quite lovely, but they also rid your home of indoor toxins. The peace lily, English ivy, and mother-in-law's tongue are also easy-to-care-for plants that remove impurities.

4. *Keep your kitchen clean.* Feng shui practitioners believe that dirty stovetops can result in the decline of family finances. I keep mine spotless, just to be safe.

5. *Store your stuff.* Clutter makes your home feel small and closed in. Try storing stuff in tubs that fit under the bed or can be stacked in the closet.

6. *Throw things out.* Donate books you don't really want and

your "low-self-esteem" clothing to your local thrift store or organize a Naked Lady Party clothing swap (see Chapter 5). Having unwanted stuff in your home is a burden.

7. *Make your bathroom a shrine.* There is a limitless amount of cheap, kitschy crap at thrift stores and novelty shops around the country. Devote your commode to bad bumper stickers (like "honk if yer horny") or outdated consumer goods (tiny trolls anyone?). My friends Liz and Stuart have covered every square surface of their bathroom with odd press clippings, ads for penis enlargements, and bizarre products. Whenever I go to their house for dinner, I make sure to use the restroom at least twice.

8. *Have a dinner party.* It will force you to straighten up.

9. *Dim the lights.* Or better, turn off all artificial light and use candles in your home. It makes it seem more dramatic and sophisticated.

10. *Breathe deeply and be grateful!* A home, no matter how messy or rundown, is a wonderful thing to have.

How to Buy Secondhand Furniture

It makes perfect sense to buy used furniture. While new furniture is very expensive, secondhand stuff is cheap; this gives you creative license. For instance, a couple of ladies in Los Angeles decided to decorate their home like a winter lodge using items found at thrift shops and garage sales. The wagon-wheel coffee table, forest landscape art, and a stuffed moose are quite convincing. Now try to get that look from Pottery Barn!

With a little know-how and planning, secondhand shopping can help you create your dream home. Here's how.

HAVE A PLAN. Start with a list of things you need. Then go through your house and evaluate items you'd like to replace. Maybe there's a pile of books in the corner that desperately needs shelves. Or your desk is ugly and you've been meaning to get a new one. Be specific. Take measurements, plan your colors, and think about periods or styles.

BUT REMAIN OPEN. Although it's important to have a plan, it's just as prudent to remain flexible. For example, say you would like a dark oak, mission-style couch with lime-green cushions. At a garage sale, you might find a mission-style light pine couch with an ugly pink fabric, but the price tag says $10. This is where your creativity comes in. You can easily stain the pine a dark walnut color and either sew new covers for the cushions or have them made. Or, because the couch is so cheap, you might even think about throwing out the cushions and buying large pillows in your color choice.

HIT THE YARDS. Once you have your list and a flexible attitude, it's time to start searching. You want to start with garage sales first because they usually offer the best deals. Consult your local paper for a list of upcoming ones. Get out your road map and set your alarm clock for 6:00 A.M.; you need to get there early. If you find something you like, don't be afraid to haggle for the best price. Inspect everything before you buy—there are no returns. You also may want to check wealthy neighborhoods near you on trash days. If you're lucky, you might just find what you're looking for.

GET THRIFTY. Once you have tried your hand at garage sales, it's time to check out the local nonprofit thrift stores (the Salvation Army, Goodwill, and other charity shops). Consult your phone book for a complete list of stores in your neighborhood. You may want to call ahead and inquire if they have furniture; not all thrift stores do.

GO ANTIQUING. After exhausting the cheaper sources, it's time for flea markets, estate sales, and antique shops (in that order). Items found at these locations will be more expensive, but they may also be of higher quality. You can find out about local flea markets and estate sales in the newspaper or online. Most cities have antique shops, although it may be worth the drive out of town, because the prices will likely be cheaper.

BE PATIENT. Don't settle! Being flexible doesn't mean going home with an item you don't like. Hold out for something fabulous. It might not be exactly what you were looking for, but it may be better!

What to Buy

Here's a list of furniture I would highly recommend getting used:

- *Metal file cabinets.* They last a long time, usually have no damage, and can be cleaned up easily. Plus, most thrift stores always seem to have at least two or three. File cabinets also are easy to find in the trash.

- *Dressers.* Why pay for that "distressed" look when you can get the real thing? With a little wood cleaner, a beat-up dresser can look nice and antique-y. You might try covering the top with a lace doily or a piece of your favorite fabric.

- *Beds.* You can find beautiful wood and metal frames and headboards at flea markets and even the occasional thrift store. Mattresses, however, are better bought new, as they can harbor bedbugs and other yucky things.

- *Bookshelves.* Unless you really hate thrifting, there is no need to buy bookshelves new. Not only are they readily available at thrift stores, you can even find them for free on the street. However, I would hold out for wood bookshelves. Even really beat-up hardwood shelving can be saved by a little sanding and a new stain or a few cans of high-gloss paint.

PAINT A PALACE

One of the easiest ways to transform your home is by painting. Los Angeles artist and crafty lady Ann Faison offers these instructions for doing it well.

EQUIPMENT

Brushes: Get good-quality brushes at the paint store. They are worth the money. Otherwise you will have bristles in your paint, which is maddening. The best brushes say "China bristle" on them. I suggest getting two large and two medium brushes and at least one small brush. One of your mediums, or both, should be angled for corners.

Buckets and trays: A five-gallon bucket with a metal screen to remove excess paint from the roller will make the job easier and cleaner if you are painting several rooms with one color. Trays and liners are better for painting with different colors and small areas. Get a couple of extra small buckets for water to clean brushes and for storing them overnight. You also will need some plastic to wrap your rollers in while a coat dries, or until the next day.

Dropcloth: Clear plastic dropcloth for carpeted rooms. Brown paper for any hard surface floors.

Heavy-duty rubber gloves: So you don't sand your fingers.

Paint: Use semigloss for doors, windows and door frames, for kitchen or bathroom walls, and for cabinets and closets. You also may want to use it for the lower half of a two-colored wall. Use flat paint for walls and ceilings in most rooms.

Piece of cardboard: To put paint cans on and thus save your floors.

Rollers and accessories: Get good-quality roller sleeves. Lambs-wool is best for latex paint. Buy a sleeve for each color, as they are not worth rinsing out. Buy two of the metal rollers so that you can switch colors without a big hassle. You also will need a broom handle if you are painting ceilings.

Sandpaper: Just get a few sheets of medium to fine. You only need rough sandpaper if you have very rough surfaces to paint, like raw or stripped wood.

Spackle and spackling knife

Tape: Rolls of wide masking tape to tape down the dropcloth.

STEP 1: GO TO THE PAINT STORE A FEW TIMES

If you follow only one piece of advice, follow this one: *Buy good paint.* There are two reasons to buy good paint: Superior paint comes in the best colors, and high-quality paint goes on easier, looks better, and lasts longer. Cheap paint is for cheap landlords and people who don't know better.

Your first trip to the paint store is primarily to pick up paint chips (those little pieces of cardboard that represent different colors) because it is imperative that you look at them in the place you are painting. Get three or four of each and tape them together so that when you get home you can have a slightly bigger area of color to look at.

Color is a mysterious thing. Because it reacts very strongly to different lighting situations, you should put your chips where you plan to paint and look at them at different times of day. Realize too that color reflects and intensifies large areas. A very pale yellow on a 2-x-2-inch piece of cardboard will become much, much deeper on an entire wall and could be overwhelming on four walls. Don't be intimidated. Intense color can be great, as long as you feel intensely about it.

While you're at the store, ask about prices. Lighter colors are usually mixed from a base of white paint and generally are cheaper (often quite a bit cheaper) than darker, richer colors. Glossy paints cost more than semi-glosses, and mattes are usually the cheapest of all. If you are on a budget, remember that all paint is not equal.

If you are painting two or more rooms, buy the paint for one room at a time. After painting the first room, you will have a much better idea of how much paint you will need for the rest of your project. You also may want to change your plans once you see how the first room turns out.

STEP 2: MOVE YOUR FURNITURE AND COVER EVERYTHING
Move your furniture into the center of the room and cover everything with tarps/dropcloths. Don't worry about the floors yet; that comes later.

STEP 3: PREP YOUR WALLS—SPACKLE, SAND, CLEAN
First, fix any little holes and cracks by filling them with spackle. (It also works on wood and plaster.) While the spackle is drying, sand down the major bumps and old paint drips. Peel off any loose bits of peeling paint, and sand those patches just enough to make a relatively smooth transition between the varying exposed layers of paint. If old paint is peeling, remove just what is already coming off. Use medium/fine sandpaper and your hands; an electric sander is overkill.

Lightly sand any enamel/gloss surfaces (door frames, window frames, cabinets and walls), roughing them up so that the fresh coat of paint has something to grab on to; otherwise it may peel.

After all your sanding is done, wipe down the surfaces with a dry cloth and then vacuum or sweep and mop. You don't want dust around when you paint.

STEP 4: COVER THE FLOOR
Put dropcloths over all exposed floor surfaces. Make sure to overlap the sheets when piecing sections together to cover a whole room. Use wide masking tape to tape the sheets to one another and to the floor. Put your paint cans and other supplies on cardboard because plastic dropcloths tear easily.

There is no need to tape window frames or moldings. It is too easy for seepage to occur, and it is simple to make a straight line along molding without tape.

Now you are ready to paint! Use a brush for edges. For large areas, use a roller in a fluid, continuous, up-and-down motion. This is the order in which you will be painting each room:

1. Edges of the ceiling
2. Middle of the ceiling
3. Edges of windows and doors
4. Edges of walls
5. Remainder of walls
6. Doors and window trim
7. Doors/cabinets

A flat edging tool with little wheels along one side is helpful for painting edges, especially for high edges, but a medium, angled brush will work just fine. Dip the brush in paint and wipe one side on the edge of the container so that one side of the brush has more paint on it. With the side that has less paint facing the surface to be painted, and the edge touching it, press the brush against the surface until a little paint gushes out. Now move the brush slowly and see what a nice clean line you get. Go along the edges of the ceiling or wall, carefully painting a straight line. Quickly wipe any mistakes with a rag dampened with water.

And that's it. A weekend project that can transform your place into a palace!

Cleaning Up/Getting Down

Like most people, I always assumed I hated housekeeping. But as I began to clean the apartment that I had so painstakingly decorated, I realized there is something lovely in the activity. I find it a relief to see instant results from vacuuming. One moment my rugs are covered with dog hair, crumbs, and dust; the next, they are clean and smooth. Same with dusting, picking up, or even washing windows. There aren't many things in life that are so immediately gratifying.

Cleaning is low-stakes work. Does anyone really care if you don't dust under each plant? No. No one will die if you don't mop, no baby will go hungry. The only person looking over your shoulder making sure you got every inch of dirt is you. (Unless, of course, you live with an extremely controlling roommate or partner, in which case you have bigger problems than dust bunnies.)

Since cleaning is inevitable for most of us, I believe it is worth finding something enjoyable in it. Mopping, dusting, scrubbing, and vacuuming help us appreciate our shelter. Cleaning is our weekly reinvestment in our home.

In searching for ways to enjoy housework, I came across the Buddhist monk Thich Nhat Hanh, who believes that cleaning can be meditative. In *The Miracle of Mindfulness* he writes: "Divide your work into stages: straightening things and putting away books, scrubbing the toilet, scrubbing the bathroom, sweeping the floors and dusting. Allow a good length of time for each task. Move slowly, three times more slowly than usual." Hanh suggests finding the sacred in everyday activities. With this approach you can meditate just by changing your intention, by breathing and moving slowly, and you don't have to live in a monastery to do it.

When it comes to the domestic, there are endless opportunities for creative approaches. Play funny music, dress in a French maid's costume, or borrow books on tape from your library to listen to while you clean. You can even try cleaning nude. It's sort of naughty and nice all at the same time. The point is to make it fun and interesting.

DIY Cleaning Products

If you are concerned about toxic chemicals in your home or are just interested in doing it yourself, it's easy to create good cleaning supplies from stuff you have lying around the house. By mixing your own cleaners, you also can save money and determine how strong they should be.

SO-FRESH CARPET CLEANER

Baking soda and cornstarch absorb dirt and odors while lavender leaves a clean, floral aroma in your carpet.

> ¾ cup baking soda
> ¼ cup cornstarch
> 3 drops lavender essential oil
> 1 Mason jar with holes punched through the lid

Combine ingredients and place in a Mason jar. Sprinkle very sparingly on dry carpet, let stand 5 to 15 minutes, then vacuum.

PRETTY ME WINDOW AND MIRROR CLEANER

It may seem odd to use vinegar as a window cleaner, but I've tested this mixture and it worked just as well or better than commercial brands on both windows and mirrors. The vinegar smell goes away after a few minutes.

3 tablespoons white vinegar

2 cups water

Spray bottle

Put vinegar and water into a spray bottle and shake to blend. Spray on windows and glass, and clean off with lots of old newspaper. Store in bottle until next use. It will keep indefinitely.

BITCHIN' BATHROOM DISINFECTANT

I love this cleaner and actually use it all over the house—on counters, plastic surfaces, and cabinets, but the place I use it most is in the bathroom. A natural disinfectant, tea tree oil is a given for the bathtub, sink, and toilet. Although the oil is expensive, a little goes a long way.

2 teaspoons tea tree oil

3 drops lavender oil

2 cups water

Spray bottle

Combine tea tree and lavender oils with water in a spray bottle and shake to blend. Shake before each use. Spray on counters and in the sink and tub. Store in bottle until next use. It will keep indefinitely.

BANISH THEE, MILDEW!

Mildew grosses me out. Please remove it from your bathtub. This simple solution works as well as those supertoxic commercial brands for a fraction of the cost.

1 tablespoon powdered environmentally friendly laundry

detergent

1 quart chlorine bleach

2 quarts water

Pail

Rubber gloves

Combine the ingredients in a pail. Wearing rubber gloves, *attack* that mildew! Afterward, rinse surface with hot water.

HIPPIE CHICK WOOD CLEANER

Even though this wood cleaner smells like salad dressing, it really does clean and care for wood surfaces. Don't worry, the vinegar smell quickly disappears.

> ½ teaspoon almond oil or olive oil
>
> ¼ cup white vinegar
>
> Glass jar with cover
>
> Soft rag

Place oil and vinegar in a glass jar and shake to mix. Dab a soft rag into the solution and wipe onto wood surfaces. Cleaner will keep indefinitely if covered; shake to combine before each use.

Share the Love

Housework is a lot more fun when it is equally distributed among all members of the household. If you live with roommates, a lover, and/or family members, consciously divide up chores. Even small children or ne'er-do-well housemates can handle a little dusting. There is nothing worse than cleaning up after others when it is not reciprocated or appreciated.

I recommend having a meeting with the members of your household to discuss cleaning. You can create rotating schedules of tasks or set aside a specific time each week to clean together. You can even make it a party. Brew a big pot of coffee and eat pastries while blasting your favorite hip-hop album. Dress the kids up in funny outfits and break out the musical soundtracks. Or play

"Bloody Marys and cowboys"—mix up a pitcher of Bloody Marys and play country western music. If you are feeling sophisticated, play classical music. Cleaning doesn't have to be terrible.

One way to relish housework is to think of it as a gift. What about offering up your housekeeping services to your best friend? The two of you could spend the day playing your favorite CDs and ridding her home of grime. Cleaning is a great way to get over a breakup, celebrate a new beginning, or just girl-bond. Cleaning house is intimate—something to share and something only a good friend would do for another.

CRAFTIVISM

There are a myriad of ways to get involved with your community around issues of "the home." Here are just a few.

- *Wages for Housework* is an international organization calling for pay equity for all work done in the home (i.e., housekeeping and child care). To get involved go to: http://www.payequity.net/WFHCampaign/wfhcpgn.htm.
- *Rural Studio.* The cutting-edge architect Samuel Mockabee and his students from Auburn University take a craft approach to providing housing for the very poor. Using salvaged lumber and bricks, old Coke bottles, and tires left for the landfills, the architects design and build award-winning houses and community centers for the impoverished citizens of Alabama's Hale County. To get involved, check out: http://www.ruralstudio.com.
- *Habitat for Humanity.* Even though it is a large organization, Habitat for Humanity actually works. They have built more than 150,000 houses around the world, providing more than 750,000 people in more than 3,000 communities with safe, decent, affordable shelter. They are always looking for crafty volunteers to help build houses. Go to: http://www.habitat.org.

3
SECOND TIME AROUND

The Craft of Thrift Shopping

When you look up the word *thrift* in the dictionary, it is identified as a noun and defined as *economy, frugality,* and *penny-pinching.* But as any crafty lady knows, *thrift* has another definition altogether. *Thrift* is also an active, creative, and crafty verb meaning to shop at secondhand stores. And a *thrifter* is someone who is perfectly happy spending an entire afternoon in a musty, dark, dank store, combing through piles of other people's throwaways. Sound enticing? It should. Thrifting is one of the great pleasures of the crafty life.

My foray into thrifting began as a teenager. In fact, purchasing secondhand clothing was an early entry into the crafty lifestyle. It worked like this: I greatly admired the tiny minority of punk girls at my Catholic school. They were boisterous, headstrong, and smart, and they could see right through the bullshit of the school

Crafty Fact. Seasoned thrift shoppers call themselves *thrifters* and use the word *thrifting* as short for thrift shopping.

administration. When they flaunted the dress code by hemming their navy blue pleated uniform skirts to micromini levels and wearing them with big, black Doc Marten boots, my interest was piqued. And when they wore "granny" dresses (slightly baggy, silk, 1940s dresses made popular by Exene, lead singer of the seminal punk band X) with high boots and ripped tights on "free dress" days, I made mental notes and tried to befriend them. My friendship wasn't reciprocated. I was way too square for their wanton ways, but that didn't stop me from copping their style. I started with baby steps, hitting first the cool vintage store called Aardvark's Odd Ark, which sold dresses like the punk girls wore. From there I ventured out to nonprofit thrift stores and crap shops all around the Southland. Garage sales and flea markets were next. And thus began my passion.

Through my admiration of these punk girls, I came to understand that what you wear can be a way of communicating who you are. People who dressed in Izod shirts and pleated beige cotton pants were *preppies*, and long-haired guys in acid-washed jeans and Ozzy Osbourne T-shirts were *heshers* (otherwise known as headbangers). I wanted my clothing to tell the world who I was. Given that I lived in the San Fernando Valley during the unfortunate era when "Valley Girl" was a huge hit on the FM dial and mall culture had reached its pinnacle, my secondhand clothing communicated a disdain for the culture of conspicuous consumption. (Think of sixteen-year-old girls driving expensive white convertibles, carrying thousand-dollar designer purses, and going on shopping splurges with daddy's credit card, and you can understand my malcontent.) I wanted to be "Alternative Girl," and I worked very hard to create a wardrobe that expressed this persona, with torn tights, vintage dresses, and asymmetrical hair.

Thrifting not only allowed me a voice of dissent (no matter how juvenile), but, more important, it offered me a creative outlet. Although I was active in the drama and art classes at school, my real creativity came out in my clothing. I created my own shirt

Pretty in Pink. If you came of age in the 1980s, chances are you've not only seen this movie, but memorized dialogue and gleaned fashion tips from its lead character, Andie, portrayed by Molly Ringwald. She wore incredible outfits throughout the movie, pieced together from thrift stores and craftiness. It's definitely good girls-night-in fodder.

designs. I sketched and planned (in hindsight) frighteningly ugly ensembles, which I wore with great pride. And I learned to think like a crafty person.

A crafty person must have the ability to see beyond an object's obvious use to create something new. Thrifting is not the gift of a skilled consumer, schooled in the latest fashions and designer wear, but the talent of an artist. In order to dress the part of a teenage provocateur, I needed to purchase my clothing for its potential, not its immediate value. This skill, sharply honed after seventeen years of thrifting, helps me add creativity to all aspects of my current life—even something as seemingly dissimilar to thrifting as cooking. For instance, when I go to the farmer's market and spot beautiful fava beans still in their shell, I don't think only about how the fava bean will taste, I envision a whole meal with the fava bean as my starting point. In my mind, I start to combine the beans with other spring vegetables, maybe some baby leeks and tiny yellow squashes, a little olive oil and a bit of fresh garlic, lemon juice, and parsley. Then I think, a roast leg of lamb, marinated in wine, oregano, and rosemary would offer a nice accompaniment to the fava bean medley. Add to that a crispy loaf of fresh-baked bread and I suddenly have an exceptional spring menu. It's the same skill that we use when we design a quilt or choose yarn for a sweater. It's called creativity, and it's a simple and delightful skill. In a world where so much can be bought easily, this kind of imagination is priceless.

Crafting and thrifting go together like peaches and cream. Ask any crafty woman and nine times out of ten she thrifts at least occasionally. Part of the explanation for this is precisely what I've been talking about: Both are creative, rather than passive, activities. But I think it also has something to do with pleasure. Part of what it means to be crafty is to enjoy life, by putting together a lovely home and a fashionable wardrobe and surrounding yourself with beauty *while doing the least amount of damage to the world.* Thrift shopping simply allows one to have more (stuff) for less (money, environmental damage, shopping guilt). You can decorate, find craft materials, and develop a unique dressing style from secondhand items and have money left over for vacations, beautiful shoes, a gourmet dinner with friends, or a donation to your favorite charity. You also can rest assured that every time you buy something from a thrift store, you are saving an item from the landfill.

Interested in proving my pleasure theory of thrifting, I set out to speak to crafty ladies about their thrifting habits. Susan, a twenty-six-year-old IT professional from Montreal, says she shops secondhand for political reasons, but she also finds much to relish about the practice itself. It seems she really, *really* loves to shop. Through thrifting, she quenches this desire without the inevitable crash that comes from overspending at the mall. By not placing money directly in the hands of big clothing manufacturers whose advertising campaigns she finds humiliating and degrading toward women, she feels free to enjoy fashion and dress up on her own terms. She also increases the quality of her purchases, by choosing good fabrics and well-made items.

For others, thrifting is an untapped resource for cheap craft supplies. Suzanne, a self-proclaimed domestic engineer from Washington, loves to find fabric at thrift stores. She writes, "What satisfaction to make a beautiful throw blanket from a couple pairs of cords, a towel, and someone's old maid-of-honor dress." When Suzanne finds a black evening gown shoved in the dusty corner of her local thrift, she doesn't just see an ugly relic from a bygone era, she identifies a fabric that might be nice in an evening purse. She uses her imagination to stretch the boundaries of the clothing itself. Again, it's about having more from less.

For Tasha, a navy wife from Fort Meade, Maryland, thrifting means the difference between having stuff and going without. Because of the low pay for new navy personnel, her family lives below the poverty line. But that doesn't stop her from approaching life in a crafty way. She states, "I can't afford nice store clothes, so

I see that the fashion wears out more apparel than the man.

—WILLIAM
SHAKESPEARE,
from Much Ado
About Nothing

all I can do is thrift." By thrift shopping, buying and selling on eBay, and finding items from the street (including a computer monitor), she is able to create a lovely home and a decent wardrobe without going into debt, something that happens to a lot of military families. With so many Americans living beyond their means (as of 2003, U.S. consumers owe a total of $1.7 trillion in debt), we could take a lesson from Tasha, who creatively pieces together a rich life from thrift stores and Dumpsters.

Some people enjoy thrifting because they feel used clothing holds a rich history of times past. My friend Kate likes to conjure up stories about the women who owned her clothes before she did. Was the former owner of her red silk shirt a Manhattan career woman in the 1970s? Did she live in one of those large white high-rises full of single women in studio apartments? Did the previous owner of her blue polyester, spaghetti-strap sundress argue with her ex and drink chablis on ice? My husband, Steve, a thrift-store dandy, has fantasies about the men who wore his suits before he did. Was the guy with the exquisitely cut navy-blue three-piece suit a closeted gay banker? Did he drink scotch on the rocks and smoke cigars in between illicit affairs with sailors? Kate and Steve's used clothing appeals to them precisely because it has history, a quality that new clothing lacks.

My own thrifting pleasure focuses on uniqueness. I love thrift store clothing because I know that when I go to a wedding wearing my secondhand, full-length, two-tiered, hand-sewn black-and-white gingham cotton dress with halter top and a black cowboy hat, no one else will be wearing it. Since the days when I admired the punk girls at my school, I've valued standing out from the crowd. Sure, if you have a million dollars, you can purchase one-of-a-kind designer dresses. For the rest of us, there are thrift stores. We crafty ladies like glamour, but we don't want to be fashion victims. Even if we had the money, we probably wouldn't feel comfortable spending $2,000 on a dress that will be out of style next year. It just wouldn't sit right.

The origins of clothing are not practical. They are mystical and erotic. The primitive man in the wolf-pelt was not keeping dry; he was saying: "Look what I killed. Aren't I the best?"

—KATHARINE HAMNETT, *fashion designer, quoted in* Independent on Sunday

A commodity appears at first sight an extremely obvious, trivial thing. But its analysis brings out that it is a very strange thing, abounding in metaphysical subtleties and theological niceties.

—KARL MARX, *from* Capital, *Volume 1*

Shopping for used clothing, furniture, and raw craft materials attracts so many of us because it is pleasurable, creative, and less harmful than any other consumer high there is. It is the Queen of Shopping.

TOP 12 THINGS TO BUY AT THRIFT STORES

1. Cashmere sweaters without holes
2. Good-quality leather belts
3. Wool coats from the 1960s
4. Little handbags from the 1950s
5. Cowboy boots
6. Glass vases
7. Champagne glasses
8. Worn-in Levi's
9. Crazy polyester jumpsuits than can be worn for Halloween
10. Candlestick holders
11. Books
12. Old eyeglass frames. You can take them to your optometrist and have her put in new lenses.

10 REASONS TO SHOP SECONDHAND

1. *Green is good.* Every time you purchase something secondhand, you support multiple uses for that item. This means less trash at the landfill.
2. *Cha-ching!* Shopping secondhand is good for the pocketbook. Even if you choose to shop at high-end consignment shops, you will pay less than if you bought it new.
3. *The cool factor.* Clothing found at thrift stores often is not available en masse, meaning that if you wear vintage to a party or wedding, you can rest assured that no one else will be sporting the same outfit as you.

4. *Serendipity.* Anyone can find a decent couch in a furniture store. But finding one at a local thrift store feels extra special and nice, especially when it's in the color that you wanted.

5. *Lady Luck!* Thrifting is like gambling; you never know what you will find. The other day my husband found a $1,200 Helmut Lang, butter-colored silk suit at the Salvation Army for $30. He was high for two days. Was he looking for a butter-colored silk suit? No. Does he love this one? Yes. Will he wear it? Absolutely. He lets luck dictate his wardrobe.

6. *Bragging potential.* Nothing makes a story like the black Gucci shoes you found at Goodwill for 20 bucks.

7. *Abundance.* If you're broke, shopping at thrift stores allows you to have more. I am a firm believer in the power of a great outfit and a decorated home to make you feel better. By shopping wisely at both thrift and consignment stores, you don't have to be wealthy to feel fabulous.

8. *Less stress.* Clothing at thrift stores is usually color coordinated and organized by shirts, pants, and dresses, a very relaxing way to shop. Plus, there are fewer items in your size and even fewer that you like, which reduces temptation to overconsume.

9. *Risky business.* Because items at thrift stores are generally cheap, you can take risks on say, a chartreuse pants suit. If you get home and hate it, at least you only spent $10.

10. *Guilt-free shopping.* Most apparel sold in this country is made by underpaid women and children in Third World countries. Thrift shopping allows us to circumvent this cycle. Instead of your money going to the Gap, it goes directly into the hands of a nonprofit organization (charities) or small businesses.

THE DIFFERENT TYPES
OF USED CLOTHING STORES

There are generally four tiers of used clothing stores:

NONPROFITS

These are your Goodwills, Salvation Armys, and the church basements. Although the nonprofits are the cheapest of the lot, you will have to dig through a lot of junk to find the gems.

VINTAGE STORES

Vintage stores are generally more expensive than the nonprofits. The advantages include a higher volume of cute and fashionable clothing, and these stores often are more organized than the nonprofits. If you are in a rush or have a special occasion to shop for, vintage stores are the way to go.

CONSIGNMENT

Consignment shops focus on high-end designer wear that is a few seasons old. You can find labels like Prada, Versace, Gucci, and others, slightly worn, for less than half the original price.

EBAY

eBay is a great place to buy used items, from office equipment to furniture to designer clothing, particularly if you live outside of a large urban area. The quality of goods runs the gamut, as do the prices and values, so always double-check prices against what you would pay to buy them new.

THRIFT TRICKS

Before you set off thrifting:

- Don't drink too much coffee or water before you go thrifting; bathrooms may be scarce.

- Go during the week. Thrift stores rarely put out new merchandise on the weekend, so if you can go before Saturday rolls around, you have a greater chance to get the good stuff.
- Go early and go often. If you must thrift on the weekend, get there right when the stores open, to make sure you have the best selection. Although it requires dedication, the best way to thrift is weekly.
- Be kind. Make eye contact and say hello to the workers when you walk in the door. Don't throw things on the floor or leave things in the dressing room. Be courteous! Aside from good karma, thrift etiquette sometimes can result in salespeople setting aside great merchandise for you.
- Bring a tape measure to make sure things fit. Unless you have a good tailor or you yourself are an expert sewer, skip items that are too big, too short, or too tight.
- Bring packets of moistened towelettes to clean your hands once you're done. Thrift shops can be very dirty places.
- Be discerning about stains.
- Dress appropriately. Many thrift stores do not have dressing rooms. Wear clothing that you can try things on over. Leggings and a tank shirt or dresses with full skirts that offer enough room for trying on pants work well.
- Go well fed. You need your energy and creativity to be flowing.
- Take care of your thrift clothing. Don't wash vintage fabrics too often; they might fall apart. Try using a brush to remove hair and lint. Airing out cotton, wools, and silks overnight often will remove odors. Machine washing and dry cleaning are very hard on clothes, and should be used only when absolutely necessary.

STEVE'S STAIN REMOVING TIPS

My husband is a prodigious thrifter, with an exceptional eye for detail. His look, which I call La Dolce Vita, is created by 1940s sport jackets, hand-tailored (for someone else) suits, and fitted dress shirts, embellished with silk handkerchiefs and over-the-top ties. In order to keep up his impeccable look, he wakes up early to iron his shirts and press his pants. And he has become an expert stain-remover. He shares some of his tips below.

TIP #1: KNOW BEFORE YOU BUY. Make sure you inspect clothes for stains at the thrift store. If you do find a stain, the first thing to do is figure out what caused it. If it's dark red, it's probably a wine stain, and chances are it is permanent. But many stains can be eliminated, including those caused by food, dirt, grease, and ring around the collar. One way to determine if the stain will come out eventually is to wet your finger with saliva and rub it on the offending area. (Make sure you don't stick the same finger back in your mouth.) Does it lighten up or smudge? If so, the mark probably will wash out later. If the stain doesn't flake off or smudge, there's still a chance it'll come out. If you really love the item and it's not too pricey, consider buying it and trying some stain-removal techniques.

TIP #2: START SMALL. I like to begin with the less harsh ingredients and then move incrementally up to the heavy stuff. First thing I try is a little hot water and liquid soap or laundry detergent directly on the spot. Then I rinse it out, let it dry, and take a look. You would be surprised at how effective simple scrubbing can be.

TIP #3: SHOUT. If the spot is still there after scrubbing with soap, I up the ante a bit with a water-soluble stain treatment such as Shout. Apply the product, wait about five minutes, and then go back and repeat tip #2. This also works wonders on the yellowing collars that you'll often see on secondhand shirts.

TIP #4: BREAK OUT THE BLEACH. If simple washing or spot treatments don't work and your fabric is white or colorfast and washable, you might want to try a little soak in bleach and water. (Follow directions on the bleach package to get the proportions right.) After the soak, wash the item as you regularly would.

TIP #5: GET HARSH. If neither Shout nor bleach does the trick, it's time for the nasty, chemical solvents. I like Afta. (You can buy it at the hardware store.) This stuff often works when nothing else does—especially on grease stains—but be sure to open all your windows before using it or you'll get a nasty high. Also, when using this type of solvent, be sure to blot it all around the stain, starting with a heavy application in the middle and getting lighter as you move outward. Otherwise you'll be left with an ugly ring where the solvent was.

TIP #6: REUSE. Sometimes nothing works. This happens; the stain is just too old and it set into the fabric long ago, or the spot was caused by some mystery substance that modern science has yet to dissolve. Make the best of it. You can use the fabric for a craft project, or if the stain is in an unnoticeable area, you can wear it anyway.

THE QUEENLY CLOSET

If you take up thrifting as a habit—it's rarely just a hobby—you probably also should become a prodigious closet organizer in order to compensate for your increased volume of clothing. Too many clothes, stuffed into a small closet, make dressing hectic and inhibit the creation of truly exceptional outfits.

WARNING: *Cleaning out your closet can be heart-wrenching. We often feel attached to articles that we've outgrown because they remind us of the past. We remember the fabulous party that we wore the snakeskin miniskirt to, even though it was ten years ago and we weighed ten pounds less. It's also anxiety-provoking to figure out what looks good on us. Doing so requires us to accept our bodies, to embrace our figures and adorn them as they are now. It requires self-love, which in our society can be elusive. That is where your best friend comes in. I highly recommend inviting someone who is supportive to clean your closet with you. Her job is to be helpful and encouraging, but also tough. She has to be feminist enough to encourage you to love your body, yet catty enough to tell you those pants do nothing for your butt.*

One best friend
Snacks and good beverages to get you through
Nice hangers
A few large plastic bags

Once you have your best friend and snacks in place, you should go through your entire closet to evaluate its contents. If you are in doubt about anything, simply try it on. Judge each piece of clothing on the following criteria:

- *Damaged goods?* Is it stretched out or falling apart or permanently stained? Just because you buy your clothing used doesn't mean you have to look like a slob—unless, of course, that's the look you're going for.
- *Is it flattering?* Life is too short for dresses that make your legs look stubby or shirts that make your boobs saggy. Pea green might be your favorite color, but if it makes your skin look like a mummy from a horror movie, it's got to go. If you are undecided, ask your friend to judge for you.
- *Do you wear it?* This is a big one. How many of us have a special skirt or pair of shoes that we never wear but are reluctant to give away? Regardless of its uniqueness, fine tailoring, or cool factor, if an item lives in your closet for more than one year without being worn, get rid of it. Never mind that you love the floral pattern or you paid lots of money for it. Throw it out!
- *Does it fit your lifestyle?* If you work in an office where you have to wear conservative clothing, a closet full of glitter polyester pantsuits aren't going to do you a hell of a lot of good. Likewise, if you are a new stay-at-home mom and have mostly suits in your closet, it might be time to get some denim skirts and a few easy-access breast-feeding

tanks. Your clothing needs to fit you, not the other way around.

- *Does it give you low self-esteem?* If you have gained weight recently, don't keep ten pairs of size-4 pants in your closet, just waiting for the day when you shed those fifteen pounds. That is plain torture. If you lose the weight, you can buy new things. In the meantime, embrace your new figure with properly fitting clothing.

Next, you and your friend should put together at least four outfits, two for day and two for night, that make you feel wonderful, sexy, and alive. When Laura was in college, her roommate came home one day during finals, dressed to the nines, with a full face of makeup, a stunning cotton dress, and little sandals. Her explanation: "Look good. Feel good. Do good." Your closet must have at least four full outfits (including shoes!) that live up to this motto. If you can't do this with your current closet full of clothes, make a list of items that you need. Try to purchase these things in the next thirty days.

Finally, once you have your big pile of clothing that you don't need anymore (I promise you, you won't even miss them), it's time to dump 'em. Fold and place them in the plastic bags before you have a chance to reconsider.

There are a number of places to send your old clothes. To enhance your thrift karma, you may want to donate your used goods to a local thrift store; you will also get a tax write-off for doing so. If you are strapped for cash and have designer or high-end pieces, you can sell them at a consignment shop or on eBay. If you're lazy and live in a heavily trafficked urban area, you always can place your bag of clothing out on the street, hoping some gleaner will find your bounty. Or to build community, you can throw a Naked Lady Party (see Chapter 5) in which you and your friends swap clothing.

CASHING IN ON YOUR DESIGNER RAGS

So you splurged on a pair of three-inch Mui Mui heels last season. The only problem is that you can't walk in them. What to do? Sell them at a consignment shop. It works like this: Once the shop decides it wants your article of clothing, you come up with a price together, and the shop sells it, with 50 percent of the profits going directly to you. Sounds simple, right? The trick is getting consignment shops to buy your items. They are notoriously fussy about what they will purchase. Here are some tips to help you make the most of your sales.

- *Mend everything.* Don't show up with a cashmere sweater that's missing a button or a pair of pants that need hemming. Make all repairs before you go. For best results, dry clean your clothing before you bring it in and keep it in the dry cleaner's plastic wrap. Buyers love this. It tells them you're serious and that the clothes are clean and pressed. If you don't want to fork out the cash for dry cleaning and the clothes are clean, lightly iron them, hang them up, and cover them with any extra dry cleaner's plastic you may have around the house. If you don't have the plastic, at least bring in clean and ironed clothing on hangers.
- *Be selective in what you try to sell.* Consignment shops want designer clothing. The big names go a long way to impress them. You might want to call a few consignment stores or go on fact-finding missions before your appointment.
- *See what's in style.* Do a little research on eBay or glance through fashion magazines to see what's in. You can bet the buyers are doing the same.
- *Make an appointment.* You must call first and make an appointment to see the buyer. Buyers hate drop-ins. When you do go in, dress in your coolest, trendiest, most expensive clothes. This is just plain good saleswomanship.

Developing a Crafty Clothing Style

If approached correctly, dressing can be a wonderful creative out-let, inspiring you to try different color combinations and experi-ment. It can be a great reason to take up sewing or knitting or color theory or even costume design! Unfortunately, many of us have been turned off to personal adornment by the societal pressure to be thin and the distorted view of femaleness portrayed in the media. To me, this is a great loss.

I believe that if we are willing to get crafty with our wardrobes, we can reclaim fashion as an empowering practice. How do we do this? Although it's sort of individual, I have a few suggestions. Thrifting is one way to do it: The availability of cheap clothing allows you to play around with different personas. Going through your closet with a good friend, as I suggested above, is another way. Finally, I think we can consciously put together a look so that dressing becomes an artistic endeavor rather than a lesson in self-torture.

These next few exercises are designed to help you develop a clothing style that honestly reflects who you are. In addition to some journaling, I recommend the same exercise that helped you create your space: making a collage out of glossy magazines and old books to help you visualize the look you'd like. I acknowledge that using fashion magazines, which can be seen as demeaning to women, in order to craft an alternative approach to dressing, may seem contradictory. But I offer this advice. First, make sure you have all different types of magazines to create from, not just *Vogue* and *Cosmopolitan.* Interior design, music, and art magazines can all be great inspirations. Try to include a few art history or costume books bought for cheap at secondhand stores or library sales, just to mix it up. Also, remember that you can find great ideas from contemporary fashion, without buying into the whole thin-is-in thing. As crafty ladies, we must take pieces from mainstream culture, cut them up, and repurpose them for our own use. If we see a skirt we adore in *Elle* magazine, on a teeny-tiny model, instead of dismissing it, we can buy a similar fabric and make the skirt for ourselves, in a size that actually fits. Instead of being victimized by the fashion industry, we can use it to become industrious.

CUT-N-PASTE: STYLE COLLAGE

10 (or more) magazines and a few colorful art and/or old costume design books

Scissors

Glue sticks or multipurpose glue

One large poster board

Journal and pen

Set aside an hour for this next exercise.

As I advised in Chapter 2, first create a mood. You can do this by burning candles, lighting incense, playing music, drinking wine, or opening all the windows. It is essential that you turn off the phone and tell family and/or roommates not to disturb you.

Next, go through the magazines, clipping any image that appeals to your fashion sense. It could be the color of blue cotton candy, a shiny fabric worn by a model, or a still from a Fellini film. Try not to be judgmental, just keep cutting. Once you have about thirty or so images, start to arrange them on your poster board. Experiment with different organizing principles. Maybe try placing your images in four quadrants mimicking the four seasons, or divide the piles up into night and day. Once you have a way to organize them, glue them into place and grab your journal.

JOURNAL EXERCISES

With pen in hand, answer the following questions without overthinking them.

1. What does your collage say about your personal style? Are you attracted to bright colors and floral patterns? Do simple lines and expensive fabrics draw you in? Do you like sexy clothes or conservative power suits?

2. Based on your collage, what kinds of fabrics and colors are you attracted to? If you had to create just one outfit, from head to toe, inspired by this collage, what would it look like?

3. If you had a huge budget and your ideal body, how would you dress? Describe day and night outfits, work ensembles, date dresses. Go into particulars. Spend a few paragraphs exploring this.

4. Think about a time when you felt beautiful. What were you wearing? Describe how the fabrics felt on your skin, the shoes you wore, the way your hair was styled.

5. Make a list of blocks that keep you from dressing the way you'd like. For each block, write down a solution, using the words *I could* to start each sentence. For instance:

    BLOCK: I can't afford high-end clothing.

    SOLUTION: I could explore the consignment shops in my hometown and hit the local thrift stores regularly, keeping an eye out for designer brands. I also could check out the designer area on eBay.

    BLOCK: My job is too conservative to warrant spending time and money on clothing.

    SOLUTION: I could find some daring, creative, and colorful clothes from thrift stores to wear on the weekends. As long as I stick to a budget, it wouldn't have to affect my finances negatively. I also could add a few fun accessories to my boring work clothes. It might cheer me up a bit.

    BLOCK: I'm not skinny enough for nice clothes.

    SOLUTION: I could indulge in some beautiful fabrics and sew my own clothing or have a tailor custom-make a dress to display my gorgeous, curvaceous body.

6. Make a list of ten simple things you can do this month to help you create your ideal personal style. They can be as simple as ironing the cotton skirt that's been sitting in the corner of your closet for two months or something more complicated, like buying a pattern for a new dress.

7. Create three body-positive mantras and place them in your closet, so that you see them every time you get dressed. Here are three examples:

> My body is wonderful *just the way it is.*
> I have the right to look good.
> Dressing well is my gift to the world.

Digging Trash

Trash can inspire. I was reminded of this the other day when watching the documentary *The Gleaners and I,* directed by the grande dame of French cinema, Agnès Varda. In it the seventy-two-year-old filmmaker explores the French countryside, philosophizing about consumption, trash, and art, and interviewing gleaners—people who live off the refuse of others. From Gypsies who pick through potatoes left in the fields, to gainfully employed city dwellers who rifle through garbage cans as a form of protest, to artists who use furniture and scraps left on the street as creative material, everyone she meets takes a stand on waste.

I love this film. Maybe it's because my own family comes from rural France and I recognize my grandmother Meme's (pronounced Mem-ay) stoop in the poor women gleaning for food in the fields in Millet's nineteenth-century painting *Le Glaneuses.* Maybe it's because gleaning appeals to my moral principals in a waste-not, want-not sort of way. (Meme grew up dirt poor and knew what it was like to go hungry, like so many people in Varda's film, and taught me to make soup out of old vegetables and fish bones, to eat the organ meats no one else wanted, to enjoy good food, but to never let it go to waste.) Maybe it's because I have experienced the rush of finding clothing, furniture, and electronics on the street. Or maybe it is simply love. My dog Bouckie was a product of my husband's gleaning; Steve found him, barely a year old, shivering under a car on Delancey Street in New York City.

I first discovered gleaning as a kid when Laura's little brother, Michael, started coming home with bunches of flowers, equipment, wood, and sometimes candy. He had found his treasure in the large Dumpsters that line the back of stores on Ventura Boulevard in the suburban San Fernando Valley.

One Sunday afternoon we set out on bikes, Michael ahead of us in rubber boots, Laura and I following in shorts, flip-flops, and tank shirts, our pubescent bodies alive with adventure. We hit the party-supply store's Dumpster first. Although neither Laura nor I actually jumped into the large steel green container, we stood to the side as Michael did and gladly took the coffee-stained stationery and stickers. Then it was on to the florist. I couldn't believe all the beautiful—albeit wilted—flowers that had been thrown out. We greedily picked through the piles, placing together motley bouquets to give to our mothers. Finding that stash was invigorating, a rush. I hadn't yet begun to think about the environmental ramifications of waste. My joy was a gambler's high: getting something for nothing, beating the odds. Free shit.

Years later, in my late twenties, living in New York City, my gleaning became more intense, both because my proximity to trash was greater as I spent hours walking the city streets each week and because New Yorkers seem to cycle through their stuff more often, swapping out the old for the newish at an alarming rate. As urban dwellers, we have small apartments. We don't own cars. Everything gets tossed to the curb. And while donations to the thrift stores might suffer, gleaners gain. At least 50 percent of my current furniture, plants, and appliances were found on the street.

It's not only in New York and L.A. that people are finding treasures from the trash. Chris from Oakland, California, found a

Streets with overcrowded and glittering store windows . . . the displays of delicacies, and all the scenes of alimentary and vestimentary festivity, stimulate a magical salivation. Accumulation is more than the sum of its products: the conspicuousness of surplus, the final and magical negation of scarcity . . . mimic a new-found nature of prodigious fecundity.

—JEAN BAUDRILLARD, *from* Consumer Society

working washing machine (she simply brought it home and hooked it up), a complete set of luggage, a few winter coats, kitchenware, and a lot of books in the trash. Amy from Baltimore found a Kate Spade purse and a black computer chair. Janet, a Tulsa girl, found a brown leather couch with nary a stain. The possibilities for treasure from the trash are endless.

Gleaning is crafty activity not merely because of the fun of finding something for nothing (although that's clearly a large part of the joy) but also for what we do with it once we get it home. Oftentimes the gleaner transforms the items from the trash into something new, with a use for which they were not intended. For instance, Becca, a cross-stitcher from Atlanta, found a vintage refrigerator on the street and converted it into a computer desk. Suzanne, a domestic engineer from Washington, D.C., came upon an old eight-pane window in the alley behind her house. She cleaned it up, left the hinges and latch on, and made it look distressed. Then she dug up some old black-and-white snapshots of her grandmother's house and had them matted and fitted to the panes, using the window as a big picture frame. She proclaims, "It looks so beautiful hanging above our fireplace!" Becca sees the inner desk in the vintage refrigerator just aching to come out. Suzanne glimpses the picture frame in an abandoned window. When a gleaner sees a piece of trash, her mind starts reeling. She thinks about how to distress it, notices that the hinges and latches give it a certain appeal, and starts plotting out her attack, even before she gets home.

Gleaning is visionary work. You must be able to come across a pile of wood and see that within these scraps lie the makings for a shelf to hold your CDs. You have to know that the planted tree that looks slightly brown, down, and dejected will flourish with a little love, water, and sunlight. To glean well, you must be able to look beyond something's obvious state, to abstractly conjure up a new use or purpose for the object. Like a good thrift shopper, the true gleaner must spend time imagining not what is but what could be.

To glean is to accept the abundance that the street offers. It does not follow that subsequently one must live without luxury. In fact, for me, it is just the opposite. I keep bottles of expensive L'Eau D'Issey perfume on my Dumpster-dived end table. In my closet, my prized three-inch Manolo Blahnik heels, found in the trash on Mott Street, sit side by side with the black patent leather boots that I bought new at Sigerson Morrison, a high-end shoe shop on the same block. I love the art and craft that goes into what someone's mother might call *finery*. I have no problem reconciling my inner Dumpster-diver with my luxury-item diva.

Reality check: Our trash dumps are reaching epidemic proportions. Americans generate more waste every year. In 1990 we collectively created 247 million tons of trash. In 2001 it was 409 million tons. That's almost double the amount of trash produced in ten years, and that's taking into account recycling programs! We are running out of landfill space, and there are more and more reports on the dangers associated with our dumps, including an increase in birth defects in surrounding areas and the pollution of underground water sources. Yet some stores still place barbed wire on their Dumpsters, because they don't want to give anything away for free. They would rather it rot. We need to readjust our thinking, to look at the fan that someone so recklessly threw out and think: It probably only needs cleaning. We need to think twice before we so readily trash our possessions, only to buy something similar. The truth is, most of us know that our society is overly wasteful, but we find it difficult to put our theories into practice. Gleaning is a good way to start. We should consider it sacred activity. In my world order, the gleaners shall inherit the earth.

MY GLEANER TOP 10
1. One adorable street dog
2. One pair of black suede, $400 Manolo Blahniks that fit me perfectly
3. One large, carved oak door that I made into a desk

4. Two vintage stereo speakers that have an amazing, rich sound
5. One wood end table
6. Two CD players—one of which worked only sporadically, while the other, a five-CD player, is still going strong, two years later
7. Three fans. Once cleaned of excess dirt and hair, they worked just fine.
8. One clothing steamer. Sure, it broke three months later, but we enjoyed it while we had it.
9. Two wood chairs
10. One *Valley of the Dolls* novel by Jacqueline Susann—always a treasure!

TRASH-PICKIN' TIPS

As you set off on your treasure hunt, consider the following:

- *Simply walk.* Some of my best finds have happened when I was just strolling through the neighborhood, not necessarily looking for Dumpster loot. In urban areas like New York City, people don't have space to store or transportation to the dump or local thrift store, so they leave perfectly good furniture and clothing right on the street.
- *Do the drive-by.* If you live in a suburban area, take a drive in the ritzy part of town on the night before trash day, preferably in a truck. Call the sanitation department to find out which day of the week they pick up large items.
- *Go to college.* Take a trip to your local university. Most schools let out in mid-May, and wealthy coeds leave boxes of perfectly usable pots, pans, furniture, and even stereo equipment outside the dormitories.
- *Hit the bins.* Go through your neighbors' recyclables for glossy magazines.

- *Dumpster dive.* Check out the large steel bins in back of your favorite stores. You probably should go at night or early in the morning, so you don't run into some grumpy manager who may not appreciate gleaners. Also watch out for barbed wire or food covered in bleach; these are tactics stores have used recently to discourage trash picking. On that note, I would discourage gleaning food from Dumpsters, unless you are really down on your luck or the food is placed lovingly in plastic for the express purpose of being picked out.

CRAFTIVISM

A few ideas for a kinder, gentler approach to our environment:

- *Feed the hungry while minimizing waste.* The U.S. Department of Agriculture has enacted the Good Samaritan Law "to encourage the donation of food and grocery products to nonprofit organizations for distribution to needy individuals." Check out the following groups that use these laws for good: City Harvest, http://www.cityharvest.org; Food Not Bombs, http://www.foodnotbombs.net.
- *Start a compost pile.* It saves on the amount of trash you produce and creates wonderful fertilizer for your garden. This crafty Web site can get you started: http://www.mastercomposter.com.
- *Move beyond Reduce, Reuse, and Recycle.* The three Rs just don't cut it when it comes to saving our environment. We need a whole new paradigm to think about products and waste. William McDonough and Michael Braungart, an architect and a chemist, have outlined a new design strategy where food wrappers could actually be good for the environment and cars could clean the air. Their book, *Cradle to Cradle: Remaking the Way We Make Things,* is the most hopeful book I've read in years. You can find out more about their design firm and work they are doing at their site: http://www.mbdc.com/index.htm

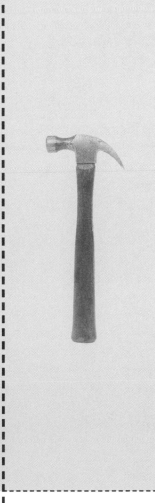

4

CONSUMING PLEASURES

Cooking as Love

Cooking is more than planning menus, shopping for ingredients, combining flavors, and creating chemical reactions. Producing a wonderful meal, while a creative and aesthetic endeavor—and, for me, a highly enjoyable activity—is also an act of great generosity. When you cook for others, you nourish and feed them. Without sounding dramatic, I would argue that when we make meals for our loved ones, we actually give them both the sustenance for life and a reason for living. To my mind, cooking is the most giving of crafts.

My grandmother Meme certainly was a generous cook. An immigrant who never lost her thick French accent, cooking was her way of communicating with the world. She worked as a personal cook for wealthy families in Paris, then New York, and, finally, Los

Food first, then morality.
—BERTOLT BRECHT,
from The Threepenny
Opera

Angeles, where she cooked for the composer Igor Stravinsky and then for the writer Aldous Huxley and his violinist wife, Laura. When Meme retired from this long life of servitude, of hot stoves and fussy madams, she grew a backyard garden and cooked for her grandchildren. You might think that after a lifetime spent in the kitchen, she would avoid cooking at all costs. Not my Meme. There were crepes on Sunday mornings, thin and crisp, drizzled with honey or, adapted for our American palate, maple syrup. Weekday meals included succulent meat loaves with slices of bacon criss-crossed on top, sautéed beet greens fresh from the garden, and brown rice. On the days when my grandparents picked me up from school, there was always fresh carrot juice and little homemade pastries.

Holidays and special occasions with my grandparents meant elaborate feasts. They always began with my grandfather Baba's famous cocktails. Baba had perfected the art of the drink during his years working at Ciro's and Mocambo's, famous Hollywood night-clubs of the 1940s and '50s, where family legend has it that Humphrey Bogart gave him the nickname "Frenchie."

As the adults consumed their drinks, I would sip my Shirley Temple and nibble on the food put out for us: salted nuts, Chinese crackers, homemade pâté, cured Italian meats, chicken livers wrapped in crisp bacon, and radishes or some other crudités. Once at the table, Meme would serve a starter like prosciutto di Parma, wrapped around juicy, cold pieces of cantaloupe or, one of my favorites, coquille St. Jacques, scallops in creamy white wine sauce, served inside large seashells. On warmed plates, my family piled slices of perfectly done roast leg of lamb, pink and juicy, with hints of rose-mary and thyme, handmade gnocchi layered with cheese and broiled until just bubbling, bowls of fresh green beans dotted with butter and parsley, and, finally, tomatoes and lettuces from the garden. After our salad, we ate cheeses imported from Normandy, the coastal area of France where our relatives had dairy farms. For dessert my Meme made Napoleons, a rich, homemade puff pastry featuring dollops of vanilla custard tucked into crisp layers. With each course, Baba chose a different wine from his cellar.

Days, even weeks, would go into the preparation of these meals. How satisfying it must have been for Meme to know she was cooking for *her* family, not someone else's. How lovely that she could sit down and enjoy the food with us, not be banished to the kitchen to eat alone while her employers dined together on her incredible dishes. How thrilling to be passing on a love of cooking and eating to the next generation.

I spent many hours in Meme's kitchen, as she lived three blocks from my parents' house, and I ate dinner with my grandparents regularly. In the afternoons I would drink tea with milk, feeling very grown up, and eat Meme's homemade madeleines, which were soft and cakelike. (I have never once doubted Marcel Proust's sensual attachment to this cookie.) As I ate and sipped, she swirled around the kitchen offering me nuggets of her wisdom, fine-tuned after a lifetime of cooking professionally. At the time, I barely listened to her advice; I was a spoiled child, the youngest of four, quite content with my croissant for breakfast, French ham and butter sandwiches for lunch, steak au poivre for dinner, and raspberries and cream for dessert. I assumed the world was full of people who would cook wonderful meals for me. When I left my Meme's warm kitchen, I realized this wasn't so. Most of my friends were raised on TV dinners and Hamburger Helper.

Miraculously, I managed to absorb some of Meme's wisdom by just being with her, like water infuses tea leaves. With reinforcement at home from my mother—a lovely cook in her own right who demanded that I start helping with the family meals when I reached adolescence—I learned how to cook. Now I find myself drawn to the magic of the kitchen. While preparing dinner, whether it's for my husband, a few girlfriends, or a group of ten, I hear my grandmother's voice helping me along. Despite my youthful brattiness, I am my Meme's granddaughter. I have inherited her passion for cooking and the sanctity of the table.

Things My Meme Taught Me

GO FOR THE FANCY

When I'm in the market and I have the choice between regular butter and a big block of organic, hormone-free, rich, creamy European-style butter that is more than double the price of the regular, I get the European-style. Meme taught me, "In order to be a good cook, you have to use the best ingredients you can find." With an exasperated expression and a blowing of the lips, she would dismiss margarine and other value brands as "sheet"—the Frenglish word for ca-ca.

WASTE NOT

Although Meme and Baba never skimped on food, they were not extravagant or wasteful. For as long as I can remember, eating at their house meant throwing apple cores in the bin headed for the backyard compost pile. Eggshells, carrot tops, coffee grinds: Everything that could be composted was thrown in there and used to feed the garden. Chicken bones and old veggies made soup stocks. For everyday dinners, Meme cooked inexpensive organ meats: tongue, brain, liver, and kidneys. Having grown up on a farm, she would never think of not eating all the parts of the animal; it was just common sense. When I would wrinkle my nose at these dishes, Meme would wave her hand in front of her face, dismissing my wasteful American ways. The biggest sin that you could commit in their household—besides eating at McDonald's—would be to throw away good food.

GROW YOUR OWN

Meme loved her garden and served her fresh herbs and home-grown tomatoes, salads, and carrots with great pride. An herb garden is a wonderful tool for the home chef. There is nothing like snipping a little rosemary for your potatoes right when you need it or adding fresh-from-the-ground oregano to your pasta sauce. If you have the time and space, a small vegetable garden will mean incredible, simple meals all summer long.

BE HEALTHY-MINDED BUT NOT RIGID

Although I've never been able to re-create her rich version of brown rice, made with chicken broth, mushrooms, and onions, I have managed to absorb Meme's emphasis on cooking food that is not only delicious but nutritious. Somewhere between the western coast of France and the hills of Hollywood, my grandmother became very interested in health foods, although never enough to forgo butter or red meat. (My brief foray into vegetarianism drove her mad.) In this way, she was ahead of her time. If she were alive today, you bet she would only buy organic and shop at the farmer's market.

EMBRACE THE LONGCUT

Cooking shortcuts, like frozen veggies and preshredded cheeses, are fine for everyday meals, when you need to prepare food very quickly. But for feasts and big occasions, you should always take the time to make it correctly. What's the point of roasting a beautiful chicken, lovingly stuffing it with fresh herbs and lemon, patiently basting it over an hour and a half, only to serve it with a canned gravy? Don't bother serving shrimp if you can't take the time to clean them well and make a fresh cocktail sauce. Meme would wrinkle her nose and stop eating at the first sign of substandard food. "Meme don't like," she would say, shaking her head in the dismissive manner that only an elderly French woman can pull off. Suffice it to say, she didn't eat out much.

FEED SADNESS

For Meme, food was solace, a tonic for all that ails you. There was nothing a fresh glass of carrot juice—the woman was juicing long before it was in vogue—or a well-cooked steak couldn't fix. Although we now consider eating out of emotional pain a psychological disorder, and certainly for some it is, eating a good meal can be healing. A simple, fresh salad, sautéed trout with a lemon caper meunière, roasted zucchini, and a crème caramel can be as comforting as a long conversation with your friends or a therapist's session. Food can be truly miraculous this way.

In our culture, we associate "emotional eating" with consuming food that is not only unhealthy, but actually makes you feel worse. Think of the depressed girl gulping down an entire pint of Chubby Hubby for dinner, while lying in bed, the phone off the hook, watching *Seinfeld* reruns. Although it might feel good going down, eating crappy food in excess, such as an entire pint of ice cream, will inevitably make you feel worse. Sugar offers a quick high with a fast and depressing crash. Combined with fat, it creates lethargy, which only leads to more depression.

Meme taught me the cure for a sad heart is delicious, healthy food. It's a totally different approach to comfort food—taking extra time to eat well when you are down, like resting when you have a cold. So the next time your best friend is blue, and you feel at a loss, try cooking for her. Include a glass of nice wine and create a meal using fresh, light, healthy ingredients. (When we are depressed, we use up more nutrients.) By dessert, you might even have her laughing. If nothing else, she will feel loved.

MEME'S MADELEINES

Madeleines are perhaps the perfect cookie. They have a cakelike interior, a slightly crispy, buttery crust, and a mellow sweetness. The rose water called for in this recipe is not necessary, but adds a subtle depth to the flavor. Stored in a plastic bag, cookies can be frozen and defrosted before serving.

There is a communion of more than our bodies when bread is broken and wine drunk.

—M. F. K. FISHER,
food writer, from
The Gastronomical Me

1 pound (4 sticks) unsalted butter, plus extra for buttering madeleine pans

3 eggs at room temperature (see note)

1 cup Superfine sugar

½ teaspoon rose water (optional)

2 cups cake flour, sifted with 1 teaspoon salt

Makes about 48 madeleines.

Double boiler

Whisk

2 large bowls

Rubber spatula

Madeleine pans (These can be purchased online at Amazon.com for under $20 each.)

Sharp knife

Cooling racks

Preheat oven to 375°.

Generously grease madeleine pans with butter.

Gently melt the rest of the butter in a double boiler. If you don't have a double boiler, improvise by filling a large pan with water and fitting a smaller heat-resistant pan or bowl on top of it. The sides of the two pans may touch, but make sure that the bottoms are separated by the layer of water.

Separate egg yolks from whites and reserve. Whisk egg whites until stiff.

In a large bowl, whip egg yolks until thick and creamy, then add sugar gradually. Slowly add melted butter to this mixture, beating with a whisk the whole time. Add the rose water, then stir in the flour until everything is well blended.

Fold in egg whites, with rubber spatula, just until incorporated.

Spoon mixture into the madeleine pans—about 1 level tablespoon per cookie.

Bake cookies on the middle shelf of your oven until edges are golden brown, about 10 minutes.

Use a sharp knife to remove hot cookies from pan and cool on racks.

Wash, dry, and regrease pans between batches.

NOTE: Bring refrigerated eggs to room temperature quickly by submerging them in a bowl of hot tap water for 10 to 15 minutes.

BABA'S DAIQUIRIS

Daiquiris are old-timey, which is what I like about them. The key to this recipe is using fresh-squeezed lime juice, to impart a true tart flavor, and powdered sugar, not simple syrup, so that the beverage has a little froth in it.

Makes 2 generous martini glasses full.

4 ounces light rum

3 ounces fresh lime juice (about 3 limes)

2 teaspoons confectioner's sugar

Cocktail shaker

Shake all ingredients with ice. Strain into a fancy martini glass.

Ideas for the Culinarily Challenged

Not everyone grew up as I did, with a chef grandmother and a mom who, even though she was in graduate school or working full-time, made sure I ate nutritious home-cooked meals each day. Frozen food in my house meant homemade lasagna that had been assembled the week before and placed in the freezer in little Tupperware containers. Fast food was vegetarian chili cooked in large quantities on the weekend and eaten throughout the week. Breakfast was not Frosted Flakes, but hot oatmeal and fresh-squeezed orange juice. But compared to most of my generation, my childhood is an anomaly. More often than not, the people I grew up with started their day with Pop Tarts, lunched at McDonald's, and munched on pepperoni pizza for dinner. I can't tell you how many of my friends don't know the difference between Cream of Wheat and cream of tartar. And if you placed a fresh, raw chicken in front of them, they might scream in terror.

If this describes you, all is not lost. I recommend that you become a one-dish wonder. What does this require? Learning to make one dish and becoming an expert at it. This way you still can feed the people in your life without having to perfect the art of cooking. For instance, my husband is culinarily challenged. When he was a bachelor, he lived off chicken tacos from a stand in the East Village and cans of corned beef hash. Since I love to cook and he does the dishes, his lack of enthusiasm is not much of an issue in our household. But there are times when I'm just too pooped to cook, or plain don't feel like it. When that happens, Steve gladly, with a bit of nudging, takes on the cooking responsibility.

Acknowledging his lack of skill, he taught himself to make an excellent omelet by reading through *Julia and Jacques Cooking at Home* (that would be Julia Child and Jacques Pépin). When I don't want to cook, he cracks eggs into a bowl with salt and freshly ground pepper and beats them until they're light and fluffy, adds them to a heated pan, and then cooks them to perfection. He serves the omelet with a tossed salad. Voilà! We have a simple dinner. It's not hard to make a good meal. All it takes is following directions and love and concern for the folks around you.

Even if you are utterly clueless in the kitchen, you still can participate in the community aspect of cooking and eating. These few suggestions will help you support your fellow cooks, ensuring that you can continue to enjoy the fruits of their labor.

- *Chop, chop.* A sous chef is the person in a commercial kitchen who gets everything prepared for the head chef and is essentially the right-hand man or woman. In a home kitchen, a sous chef is anyone willing to chop onions, wash veggies, peel potatoes, clean pans, and set the table. You don't need to know diddly-squat about cooking to be an efficient home kitchen sous chef, although a few knife skills wouldn't hurt.

- *Wash them dishes!* The last thing cooks want to do after they slaved away all afternoon is clean up. My husband, lacking the culinary skills but not the appetite for fine food, keeps himself well fed by being an expert dishwasher, not only in our home but at the homes of our friends who have us to dinner. We always get invited back.

- *Shake it up!* If all else fails, you always can learn how to make excellent cocktails. Buy a couple of how-to books and practice, practice, practice until you are proficient at making at least five mixed drinks. The next time you are invited to a dinner party, offer to make a few cocktails, assuring your host and/or hostess that you will be bringing your own alcohol, mixers, and accoutrements. Or go as far as having your own cocktail party, ordering in your appetizers and serving fancy drinks made to order.

Part of what it means to be connected to others, to be part of a community, is to give of yourself. Cooking is a simple, joyous, crafty way to do this. Eating well with people you love is incredibly pleasurable. I encourage you to make cooking and eating a priority in your life.

MY MOM'S VEGETARIAN CHILI

This recipe is fast and easy. Onions, celery, and carrots give it a fresh taste, while the cumin and chili powder make it hearty and flavorful. Best of all, it's adaptable. Every time I make this chili, I change it a bit. Sometimes I use all pinto beans instead of black and garbanzo. Other times I substitute two fresh jalapeños or canned chipolte chiles in adobe sauce and leave out the zucchini. If I have frozen corn, I add it to the pot for the final five minutes of cooking. Since I don't like bell peppers, I always omit them. Play around with this recipe to create your own favorite version.

3 tablespoons olive oil

1 large onion, chopped

1 cup chopped celery (about 5 stalks)

1 cup chopped carrots (about 5 carrots)

Salt and freshly ground black pepper to taste

3 cloves garlic, finely chopped

1 tablespoon ground cumin

2 teaspoons ground chili powder

2 15-ounce cans chopped tomatoes

1 15-ounce can garbanzo beans, drained and rinsed

1 15-ounce can black beans, drained and rinsed

1 teaspoon dried oregano

1 cup water

1 cup chopped zucchini (about 2 medium zucchinis)

1 green or red bell pepper, diced

½ cup chopped red onions

½ cup shredded cheddar cheese

⅓ cup chopped fresh cilantro

2 avocados, sliced

Sour cream to taste

Makes 6 servings.

GARNISH

In a large, heavy pot, heat olive oil on medium heat. Add onion, and cook until translucent.

Add celery and carrots, and cook another 2 to 3 minutes. Then add salt, pepper, garlic, cumin, and chili powder, and stir for 1 minute.

Add tomatoes, beans, oregano, and water. Cover and cook on low heat for 30 minutes.

Add remaining vegetables and cook for an additional 5 minutes.

Top each serving with red onions, cheddar cheese, cilantro, avocado, and sour cream.

Cooking Outside the Lines

Although cooking is often an act of generosity, a wonderful side effect is that when you cook, you are master of your universe. Sure, there are lots of rules and culinary traditions, but you don't have to follow them. Once you learn the basics, you are free to experiment. In fact, some of the most exciting chefs break the laws of cooking and invent new dishes. With very little practice, you can learn to follow your own tastes and senses in the kitchen. I call it cooking outside the lines. It's sort of like traveling without a guide book; sometimes the results are disastrous and you end up sleeping in a train station (or, in the case of cooking, throwing out the entire pot), but often you find yourself in amazing, unexpected places.

Here are some ideas to get you started:

- *Know before you go.* Learn the basics of cooking. You can do this in myriad ways. Take a cooking class, watch the Food Network, or study a few cookbooks. The *Joy of Cooking* is a truly great beginning cookbook. It covers everything from slicing and dicing to boiling water and making coffee.
- *Taste everything.* Once you know the basics, you're ready to go nuts. (Excuse the pun.) I recommend setting aside some time to have a tasting party. Spend an hour going through all your herbs and condiments. Taste red vinegar, white vinegar, apple cider vinegar. How do they differ? Put dried oregano on a bit of ricotta cheese. How is this different from dried basil? Taste soy sauce, miso, Thai fish sauce. Put ketchup on your tongue. Is it sweet, or salty, or both? Are the flavors warm or cool? Are they acidic or rich? Is the heat of the chili sauce sort of smoky, or is it tart? Imagine what they could accompany. Could chicken stand up to the intensity of chipotle peppers, or is steak more in order? What

about the chutney in the back of the fridge? Might be nice with pork chops and caramelized onions. Maybe that cumin could spice up some potatoes and create a taco filling. Take notes and commit to trying out some of your ideas.

- *Be postmodern.* Think of your favorite dish and deconstruct what works about it. For instance, if you adore guacamole, explore what it is about this dish that is so appealing. I like guacamole partly because it is green, which always signifies freshness to me. It's also creamy, with little bits of onion and jalapeño crunch. It's rich, salty, and a little spicy. There's often a bit of acid in it, maybe a lemon or lime, to cut the richness. Now, what other combinations could give you some of the same experiences? Maybe you have some frozen peas on hand. How about doing what Laura's mom does: Blend the peas with salt, lemon juice, and olive oil to create a pea guacamole? If you have a bunch of potatoes, could they benefit from a similar approach? Trust your instincts and go by what flavors and textures you really crave.

- *Think globally.* Don't be afraid to cook cross-culturally. Use ingredients from different countries together by tasting and experimenting. Who knows, maybe Vietnamese chili sauce goes great on tacos. Or maybe Nori could benefit from tuna salad. This kind of cooking, called fusion cuisine, is quite popular. Chefs combine Brazilian and Japanese, Asian and Mexican, Chinese and Cuban foods. If they can do it, you can too.

- *Salt and pepper.* Don't be afraid to use salt and pepper. Salt really improves the flavor of foods. Black pepper adds not only flavor, but a bit of heat and rounds out a dish. Red pepper flakes can add spice and layers of intensity to otherwise ordinary foods.

- *Indulge.* Fat adds flavor, which is why famous TV chef Emeril Lagasse likes to exclaim: "It's a pork-fat thing!" When used wisely, butter, lard, and olive oil can really expand your repertoire. Alas, fat is full of, well, fat, but it's also delicious!

- *Relax.* If anything goes horribly wrong, you always can order in and chalk the mess up to research.

All Lost in the Supermarket

Another way to bring some creativity into the kitchen is to approach grocery shopping from a tourist's point of view. When you're in a foreign country, it's always fun to go to the grocery store and check out all the different foodstuffs they have, but we rarely explore the plethora of items we have access to domestically.

Instead of shopping directly from your grocery list, why not try buying all new products? For instance, if your list usually calls for hot cocoa, instead of buying Nestlé or some other standard brand, try Mexican hot chocolate or even carob powder. Instead of milk from cows, buy almond milk. Replace standard pinto beans with Italian Roman beans. Instead of regular pasta, try Faro. Trade steak for buffalo meat. Replace onions with shallots and so on. By shopping outside of your normal ingredients, you can expand your cooking repertoire, try new recipes, and even develop new favorites. Most important, you break out of your cooking rut.

Be the Hostess with the Mostest

I have thrown many a dinner party in my day. Some were great, like the Valentine's dinner I made last year. We started with champagne and oysters, dined on braised short ribs, wilted greens, and wild rice for our main course, and finished with fine chocolates and fresh strawberries. The food came together perfectly, the meat was fragrant and tender, the greens had just the right amount of bitterness, and the strawberries and chocolate were the perfect ending to a rich meal. The guests got along famously, and we had great conversations.

Some dinners, though, were awful. The Thanksgiving of 2000 comes to mind as a major disaster. The meal took two days for my husband, me, and our niece Lila to prepare. We shopped, chopped, and cooked until we were exhausted. On Thanksgiving, we overcooked the turkey and the stuffing came out greasy. I got in a fight with a good friend, and, if that wasn't enough, our dog bit one of the guests. By the end of the meal, I was packing up leftovers into plastic containers and trying to get our guests to leave so I could sulk in the bathtub.

After such an ordeal, why would I ever entertain again? Because a dinner party is a great way to practice the generosity of cooking and to build community. When done correctly, it makes you feel warm and tingly all over. It's about sitting around with your friends, wiping the salad dressing left on your plate with bread, and arguing politics. It's about having another glass of wine and saying, "Remember that time when . . ." It's about feeling you belong somewhere.

A good dinner party is kicked back enough so that people feel free to slouch at the table, with food that leaves everyone satisfied and just enough drink so that conversation is easy. If the host/hostess is relaxed, then everyone else will follow suit. This is very important. Don't put too much pressure on yourself to make everything perfect. "Good enough" should be your motto. Below are a few things I've learned over the years.

PARE DOWN YOUR INVITES

A dinner party should be a small, intimate affair, with a maximum of eight guests. A bigger guest list is fine for a barbeque or drinks and appetizers, but a dinner party must be small in order to stay focused on food and conversation.

CREATE A MOOD

There is a reason that fine restaurants spend thousands of dollars on décor: Eating in a lovely, thoughtful space makes food taste better. When you throw a dinner party, your home should feel just a little different, a little special. You want your guests to walk in and instinctively understand that this is an occasion. It can be as simple as cleaning the house and lighting a few candles or playing music that matches the food you are serving.

DECORATE THE DINING ROOM TABLE

If you have a dining room table, decorating it can be an effective mood enhancer. You can drape the table in a beautiful piece of fabric and throw rose petals down the center. Or you can use herbs as table decorations: Laura recently created small centerpieces out of miniature potted parsley plants. She wrapped their plastic green containers in burlap, which was kept in place with kitchen string. You also could consider making name cards for your guests, which tell everyone where to sit and make you social engineer for the evening. Fresh flowers, colored napkins, or inspirational sayings written on note cards and placed on each plate can help make the occasion festive. Experiment with color, sound, and light.

DON'T BE AFRAID TO BREAK THE RULES

Just because you don't have a table doesn't mean you can't throw a dinner party. I once spent an evening in a graduate student's tiny apartment where we all ate squished together on the couch with our plates on our laps. Our drinks were set on the coffee table. The hostess had lit candles everywhere and displayed two huge bouquets of flowers for atmosphere. We ate perfectly cooked duck and wild rice and a great big tossed salad for our main course. The conversation and food was exquisite, although getting up to go to the bathroom was difficult. But eating this way made the experience feel all the more bohemian.

USE REAL PLATES

No matter how you are serving your meal—on a grand oak table or on the living room rug—you should use real plates and silverware. Save paper plates and plastic forks for your barbecue. If you don't have plates and cutlery for all of your guests, pick up some at the thrift store—it's not like they have to match!

GET HELP

Don't have time to go to the thrift store for extra plates? Ask one of your guests to bring them. It's perfectly respectable to ask people to bring cutlery, dessert, wine, bottled water, or even appetizers. Helping out, by bringing something or even serving dishes or cleaning up afterward, is a way for folks to feel included. Contributing to a dinner party can help those who are a bit shy move from awkward guest to an integral part of the party itself.

PLAN AHEAD

If you can, make most of the food before your guests arrive, so that you don't have to stress getting everything together at the last minute. You may want to start early the morning of the party and devote the entire day to cooking—going slowly, taking your time, maybe even sipping a little glass of wine and listening to a favorite album. That said, if you find yourself cooking at the last minute, don't fret. There's nothing worse than showing up for a dinner party with the hostess running around with her panties in a bunch because the meal is not ready. If you calm down and just keep cooking, everything will be okay. Last-minute cooking even has its benefits. Your friends may come into the kitchen to talk to you while you work and offer to help. Having everyone work together can create a more relaxed vibe to the meal.

THE POWER OF APPETIZERS

One trick to dinner party success is having appetizers and drinks ready as soon as the guests arrive. It gives everyone something to do before the dinner is served, and it's a nice ice-breaker. Plus, if you are behind with your cooking, at least the guests won't starve.

Don't fuss with appetizers and drinks. Just keep it simple, with flavors similar to your main course. Serving enchiladas? Offer margaritas as a cocktail and guacamole and chips as an appetizer. Assign a friend to be in charge of serving the drinks and keeping the appetizer bowls full, so you don't have another thing to worry about.

GO FOR AN EASY MAIN DISH

Unless you have been to cooking school, spent time in a restaurant kitchen, or grew up cooking for a large family, you might want to focus the main course around one simple, hearty dish, like a baked ham or braised short ribs. Vegetarians could assemble some sort of vegetable and cheese casserole.

While the main course is cooking, you can prepare a few side dishes. For instance, with baked ham you may want to serve collard greens and three-cheese macaroni. With braised short ribs, baby red potatoes, fork-smashed with a little butter and parsley, and crisp green beans would be nice. And with the veggie casserole, I'd go for a big mixed green salad, with walnuts, dried cranberries, and ricotta salata cheese.

MAKE DESSERT DIFFERENT

If you don't want to make dessert and you're too broke to buy a fancy tart from the local bakery, you can serve fresh fruit; a few pears or even berries are nice at the end of a big meal. You also can go with frozen desserts. In a pinch, my friend Gayle likes to serve dulce de leche ice cream with a garnish of sliced Granny Smiths for a makeshift candy apple.

DON'T FORGET THE TOAST

It's kind of silly, but I like starting my meals with a toast. It creates community and sets the tone.

Last-Minute Meals

Below is a list of favorite ideas for last-minute meals. The dishes are made from simple, uncomplicated ingredients. These recipes are for the days when you come home from work tired and hungry and need to throw something together in less time than it would take the delivery guy or gal to get there. Or for when friends just happen to drop by unannounced on a Wednesday at 7:00 P.M., hinting that they'd like to stay for dinner. Last-minute meals are designed to be full of flavor and attitude with a Miles Davis improvisational flair, rather than a Bach symphony of highly orchestrated tastes. In other words, you can easily substitute ingredients to suit your tastes or your cupboard. These recipes are meant to be a starting point for your fun.

PASTA WITH PANCETTA, CAPERS, AND BROCCOLI RABE

This pasta is a delightful break from "pasta with red sauce." Broccoli rabe has a distinctively bitter flavor, which the pancetta plays nicely against, but you could easily substitute any dark leafy greens in this recipe. When I have vegetarian friends over, I just leave out pancetta and add extra capers.

Serves 2 with leftovers.

1 box farfalle pasta (or similar shape)

SAUCE

2 to 3 slices pancetta or bacon

½ medium onion, chopped

1 clove garlic, minced

1 bunch broccoli rabe, washed, tough stalks removed, and chopped fine

5 to 10 capers

½ teaspoon dried red pepper flakes

2 tablespoons olive oil

¼ cup grated Romano cheese

Put water for pasta on to boil.

Fry pancetta or bacon in a large skillet. When done, remove from heat and drain on paper towels. Drain fat from pan, except for 1 tablespoon. (Vegetarians: Omit bacon. Use 1 tablespoon olive oil here.)

Sauté onion in skillet until it begins to turn translucent. Add garlic and broccoli rabe and cook on medium heat, adding a few splashes of water if garlic starts to burn. Cook until broccoli rabe is tender.

Return pancetta or bacon to skillet and add capers and pepper flakes. Turn off heat, drizzle the olive oil over the broccoli rabe, and cover.

Cook pasta according to the package instructions. When pasta is done, drain, add the broccoli rabe and Romano cheese, and toss well.

MEXICAN BREAKFAST

I love making eggs and beans for breakfast; it reminds me of growing up in Southern California. This dish is high in calories but well worth it. It's also the perfect beer-sop for the morning after a long evening out.

1 clove garlic, minced

1 fresh jalapeño pepper, sliced and seeds removed

½ medium onion, chopped

2 tablespoons canola oil

1 8-ounce can pinto beans, drained and rinsed

4 to 6 corn tortillas

4 eggs

3 slices bacon, cooked well done and crumbled

½ avocado, sliced

Fresh cilantro

Bottled hot sauce (I recommend Tapatia brand)

Serves 2 very hungry people.

Sauté garlic, jalapeño, and onion in oil until onion is translucent. Add beans and mash with a potato masher or fork. Add a small amount of water if the mixture seems too dry. Cover to keep warm.

Heat the corn tortillas in a cast-iron pan or simply place them directly on your gas stove's burner on a medium flame, flipping with kitchen tongs. If you have an electric stove, you can steam tortillas in a bamboo steamer or wrap them in aluminum foil and heat them in a 350° oven. Keep heated tortillas warm in a clean kitchen towel.

Fry the eggs over-medium.

While eggs are cooking, arrange 2 tortillas on each plate and top with bean mixture. Place 2 eggs per person on top of bean mixture, then sprinkle with crumbled bacon. Garnish plates with avocado slices and a few sprigs of cilantro. Serve with hot sauce and extra tortillas.

Quick Ideas

Here are some more tips for quick, easy meals:

- When friends pop by on a Saturday afternoon, serve an appetizer plate and a bottle of wine. Arrange olives, slices of rolled ham, cheese, and crackers on a plate and open some Merlot. Sounds simple, but your friends will be impressed.
- To make a quick dinner, boil, drain, quarter, and toss potatoes with parsley, chopped hard-boiled egg, olive oil, and vinegar for a warm potato salad. Serve on top of mixed greens.
- For an even quicker dinner, toss mixed greens with one can of cannellini beans, one can of high-quality tuna packed in olive oil, and a balsamic vinaigrette. Presto—you've got a great meal.
- For dessert try a healthful and easy yogurt sundae. Top plain or vanilla yogurt with chopped dates and walnuts and drizzle with honey. It's surprisingly satisfying.

A FEW BASICS

Here is a list of things I like to always have in the house. You might want to create your own list and put it on the door of your fridge, so you can create your shopping list easily each week.

Good olives

Crackers (I like Stone Ground Wheat Crackers.)

Cheese: A simple cheddar is always appreciated, especially with a few slices of green apple. You also can try goat cheeses on salad. Don't be afraid to experiment with cheese! A Spanish Manchego with bread and tomatoes can make an excellent lunch, and ricotta salata in a salad with a few dried cranberries can be heavenly.

Parmesan and/or Romano cheese is a must for pastas or even on top of sautéed greens. You can buy it pregrated and keep it in the freezer, although nothing beats grating it fresh.

Almonds or walnuts

Potatoes (I like small varieties like Yukon Gold or fingerling, which have more flavor and cook quickly.)

Mixed salad greens (I usually buy them prewashed.)

Parsley

Garlic

Onions

Good olive oil (I like Colavita brand.)

Good balsamic vinegar

Dates

Whole-milk yogurt

Good butter

Pancetta or bacon

Sliced French ham

Cans of stewed tomatoes

Organic chicken broth

Brown rice

Capers

Cans of pinto beans

Good tuna packed in olive oil

Organic eggs

Dry pasta

Eating and the Single Girl

For six years of my life, I lived alone. From that period, I understand what the German philosopher Walter Benjamin meant when he wrote "Taking food alone tends to make one hard and coarse." Like most Americans, I spent a fair share of my mealtimes in front of the TV, consuming tuna from the can or takeout directly from the white paper container, eating without really tasting. Why did I do this when I obviously love food? Mostly because there is something counterintuitive about cooking an elaborate, multi-ingredient meal for yourself. It seems like such a waste of time to do all that work for a small moment. When cooking for one, the main motivation of cooking, sharing, is gone. There is no praise, no reward, and no one to enjoy the glory with you. No one is there to say "Mmmmm, this is excellent! How did you make it?" Because food is such an intrinsically social experience, it takes a lot of effort to treat yourself to a well-cooked meal.

As an experiment, for the last couple of years of my single-girl tenure, I got rid of my television and set out to not only cook for myself, but to eat without distraction. I discovered that Walter Benjamin was, if not wrong, contextual. It was not eating alone that made me coarser, but rather eating unconsciously, without pleasure. Once I set my mind to it, meals, even meals spent alone, made me feel more grounded and homelike in my tiny tenement apartment.

I also decided to take my lunch to work everyday, which meant, of course, more cooking, but in a different manner from how I had prepared food in the past. I learned to do what busy moms have done for decades: I cooked in batches. Instead of baking one cornmeal-coated chicken breast for dinner, I made three, so that I could have it for lunch over the next two days. I tossed large salads and stored them in single-size plastic bags and bought a bottle of my favorite dressing to keep in the office fridge. I shopped for good cheese, crackers, olives, and other easy foods, which could always be packed at the last minute. Cooking three or four meals at a time actually made me more excited to make dinner; there is something satisfying about getting four for one—it's what entices us to buy three on-sale deodorants in a scent we don't even like.

I also found consumer satisfaction in my grocery shopping forays: Not only is spending money on food a guilt-free exercise, but it sparks the imagination and makes cooking and eating all the more exciting. It must be how a painter feels when she goes to the art-supply store, surrounding herself with colors and brushes, ripe with possibilities. Roaming the aisles of the food stores, I discovered the new Basque cheese or located the freshest asparagus or the most fragrant strawberries and felt compelled to cook. Once home I turned on a Chet Baker CD, made myself a beautiful plate of food, and slowly enjoyed the flavor and textures, all by my lonesome. I finally understood the food writer M. F. K. Fisher's preference for dining alone. As she points out in her book *The Gastronomical Me*, "sharing food with another human being is an intimate act that should not be indulged in lightly."

CRAFTIVISM

There are a plethora of opportunities to get involved in changing the world through food. So many issues need our attention: child obesity, malnutrition and hunger, the proliferation of genetically engineered food, the environmental ramifications of agribusiness practices, and the globalization of the American fast food diet. Here are just a few things you can do to make a difference.

- *Buy organic.* Simply choosing to buy foods that are produced organically has a positive effect on the environment, farmworkers, and you. Many grocery chains have started to carry organic produce and chicken. If you can, shop at local farmer's markets, where you will support local farmers. Although it's not always possible, convenient, or affordable to eat organically, every effort counts.
- *Join a CSA.* According to a recent survey by North Carolina State University, 77 percent of those polled agreed that government policies should favor family owner-operated farms as opposed to those run by

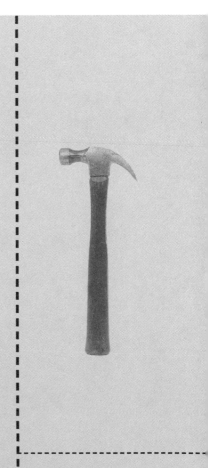

corporations and 53 percent prefer to buy food they know has been grown on small rather than large farms. Unfortunately, our government takes the opposite position, giving huge subsidies to large agribusinesses whose bottom line is profit, not your health. CSA stands for Community Supported Agriculture; CSAs offer consumers an opportunity to act according to their beliefs. By paying a certain amount to a working farm every year, consumers help the farm stay afloat and guarantee buyers for the farm's produce. In return, consumers receive fresh, farm-raised organic food delivered to a nearby location or directly to their home. It's a very simpatico relationship, although it's not without risk. Since consumers invest directly in a specific farm, a bad harvest will mean less food on your table, but even this risk has its benefits. It reminds us of our connection to the earth. The Organic Consumer Association contains a list of CSAs throughout North America: http://www.organicconsumers. org/csa.htm.

- *Start a Slow Food convivium.* Founded in Italy during the 1980s, Slow Food is an organization devoted to guaranteeing fresh, local products and retaining a culture where sitting down and enjoying these foods is viable. It is the political, pleasure-filled response to the worldwide proliferation of American fast food and global agribusinesses. The goal of the organization, which currently boasts 65,000 members in Argentina, Austria, Brazil, France, Germany, Holland, Hungary, Japan, Spain, the United States, and Venezuela, is to protect the historic, artistic, and environmental heritage of foods *and* to literally slow down to enjoy them. Slow Food is against food that has been genetically modified or manipulated and in favor of organic farming and biodiversity. One of the ways the movement spreads its message is through the grassroots organizing of political eating clubs called *convivia*. A *convivium* is a small local organization that brings people together for wine and food events and raises the profiles of local products and produce. To find or start a local chapter of Slow Food, go to: http://www.slowfoodusa.org.
- *Help grow an Edible School Yard.* The original Edible School Yard is the brainchild of Neil Smith, principal of Martin Luther King Junior Middle School in Berkeley, California, and renowned chef Alice Waters of Chez Panisse. The students at this school, working with faculty, grow their own

vegetables and then learn to cook meals with their bounty. The goals of the program are manifold: to encourage children to eat healthful, nutritious foods; to create a more holistic and practical learning environment by incorporating food and recipes into lesson plans; and to teach life skills, such as cooking and growing food and ecological awareness. This is a wonderful program that can have real lasting effects on future generations. For information on how to start an Edible School Yard in your community, go to: http://www.edibleschoolyard.org.

- *Feed the Needy.* One of the goals of Craftivism is to change the world through arts and crafts. Working at a soup kitchen, chopping, peeling, and cooking for those less fortunate than you, is a way to use your creativity to make a change. Many great organizations operate soup kitchens. The best way to find them is to search online for local churches that feed homeless people or AIDS and cancer organizations that deliver food directly to the sick and needy. In New York, one of my favorite soup kitchens is God's Love We Deliver; go to: http://www.godslovewedeliver.org.

Resources

FOOD READS

Reading is a wonderful way to gain inspiration in the kitchen. But we don't have to limit ourselves to cookbooks. A number of novels, essays, and memoirs revolve around food and include, if not recipes, then thoughts and descriptions of beautiful meals woven into engaging stories. Here are some of my favorites:

The Art of Eating by M. F. K. Fisher

A collection of essays by perhaps the greatest American food writer. With the culinary arts as its starting point, the essays document Fisher's life in Europe, her loves and passions. Required reading for foodies.

The Book of Salt by Monique Truong

The location is 1934 Paris and the story belongs to Binh, cook for Gertrude Stein and Alice B. Toklas. The novel follows Binh's narrative from French-colonized Vietnam to the center of America's Lost Generation. It contains beautiful prose about cooking, love, and the loneliness of exile.

Comfort Me with Apples by Ruth Reichl

A food memoir from the editor of *Gourmet,* this book tells the second part of Reichl's coming-of-age story, from Berkeley bohemia to successful New York food writer and editor. Although she abandons Northern California, Reichl never loses her counter-cultural edge nor her honesty, which is what makes this book so delicious.

Fast Food Nation by Eric Schlosser

A must-read for anyone who is concerned with nutrition and the environment. Schlosser is an engaging writer, and his prose is never dry or boring. He follows the history of fast food chains, from mom-and-pop stands to multinationals, and traces the expansion of agribusiness and the rise in U.S. obesity. After you read this book, you will never look at a Big Mac in the same way again.

It Must've Been Something I Ate: The Return of the Man Who Ate Everything by Jeffrey Steingarten

A very funny, well-written collection of essays from an obsessed gourmand, who will do anything for a good meal, including smuggling horse fat into the United States in order to make proper French fries.

The Passion by Jeanette Winterson

This novel is a favorite among many women I know. The book centers on Henri, who is sent to fight in the Napoleonic wars and becomes the cook for Napoleon himself. Henri's story smacks into the story of Villanelle, a cross-dressing Venetian woman born with webbed feet. Although not a typical historic novel, the book weaves through time and reality with the lightest of touches. This is a great read-it-in-one-weekend kind of book.

The Patron Saint of Liars by Ann Patchett

Rose, a born liar, gets pregnant, ditches her husband and her confining marriage, and goes to live in a Kentucky home for unwed mothers. Once there, she keeps her baby and becomes the cook, living out most of her life in the kitchen. Through cooking she maintains her sanity, even while she continues to live a life of deception. Told from three different perspectives, the novel is rich with the sorrow of mistakes and human frailty.

MY FAVORITE COOKBOOKS

The following are cookbooks that I consistently use, whose recipes never fail to delight me. They are a great beginning to any cookbook collection.

Chez Panisse Vegetables by Alice Waters

Alice Waters is a patron saint of craftiness. The owner of the famous Chez Panisse in Berkeley, California, she single-handedly transformed American cooking in the 1970s by focusing on extremely fresh, organic vegetables and meats. The recipes in this cookbook sparkle with creativity and panache. They are also simple enough for the home cook to follow, unlike some chef's cookbooks.

Julia and Jacques Cooking at Home by Jacques Pépin and Julia Child

I am forever fond of these two, not only for their great cooking skills, but also because I like their relationship: a younger French professional chef and an older American home cook shouldn't get along so well. This book offers excellent French recipes with detailed instructions and photos, taking you through the entire process, step by step. More important, the authors usually offer two ways to do things: one from each chef, along with the reasoning behind their different approaches. This is helpful because it not only provides alternative ways to cook the same dish, but shows you how personal cooking is.

Essentials of Classic Italian Cooking by Marcella Hazan

My husband and I have two friends, Stuart and Liz, who both are college professors and food lovers. Stuart is known for his incredible cooking and his signature dish, osso buco. So when they bought Steve and me this cookbook for our wedding, I couldn't wait to dive in. Hazan's pure, simple recipes for pasta, vegetables, and meat will make you rethink what you consider Italian food. Many dishes are easy to make but require good, fresh ingredients. Her recipe for pasta Bolognese is one of my favorites.

The New Joy of Cooking by Irma S. Rombauer, Marion Rombauer Becker & Ethan Becker

A classic, standard cookbook with thousands of recipes and explanations for everything from cuts of meat and the best way to blanch vegetables, to the importance of a candy thermometer.

FOOD BY INTERNET

Thanks to the World Wide Web, it is possible to order finely crafted, specialty foods from small farms or far-off countries and have them delivered directly to your door. Here are just a few of the excellent foodstuffs that are out there.

BACON-OF-THE-MONTH CLUB

"I'm one of those crazy people who believe that good food and wine have the power to heal," says Dan Phillips, creator of

gratefulpalate.com. In addition to a campaign to be the first person to send bacon into space, Dan hosts a bacon-of-the-month club. One package of hand-picked artisan bacon, chosen from the finest purveyors around the world, is delivered to your door each month, for an entire year. The Grateful Palate also features wine, honeys, preserves, and other artisanal products.
http://www.gratefulpalate.com

Get Cheesy

If you lack a good cheese shop in your neighborhood, it may be worth visiting igourmet.com, an international cheese Web site. I have used their services for both gift baskets and to sample hard-to-come-by cheeses and have been pleased on both occasions. For a dinner party, nothing can beat an exotic, flavorful cheese such as Italian Piave Vecchia, a nutty, hard cheese served as a simple appetizer, accompanied by crusty bread and red grapes.
http://www.igourmet.com

Some Like It Hot

For chipotle peppers in adobo sauce, which contribute a wonderful smoky flavor to pozole, and other Mexican ingredients like hot chocolate, check out MexGrocer.com. Special bonus: They also sell inexpensive seven-day votive candles, which, when personalized with photos and sayings, make marvelous gifts.
http://www.Mexgrocer.com

Coffee Buzz

Many coffee connoisseurs say that Distant Lands coffee is the best available in the United States, because the company does not over-roast the coffees. The price per pound is cheaper than Starbucks and comparable to most high-quality beans.
http://www.dlcoffee.com

MEAT TREATS

Pretend you're a cowgirl by ordering your meat from the Wild West. Niman Ranch features excellent quality beef, lamb, and pork, grown without harmful additives or hormones. Besides being incredibly PC—the animals are all humanely raised and fed on a grain mixture that contains no animal by-products and no genetically modified ingredients—the taste of Niman Ranch meat is like nothing else you've experienced. The care and time taken to raise the animals means tender, well-marbled meats, which are created for superior taste and texture, not a fast buck. Their prices are more expensive than that hormone-laden stuff you get wrapped in plastic from your local grocery, but it's worth every penny, especially for a special occasion. You can order online, and Niman Ranch will FedEx the meat directly to your front door. http://www.nimanranch.com

BE PEACHY

Sadly, it's difficult to find a good peach these days. Luckily, Frog Hollow Farm grows luscious, juicy, organic peaches, available only in the summer months. It delivers anywhere in the continental United States. They also sell fruit preserves and chutneys. http://www.froghollow.com

5
NO WOMAN
IS AN ISLAND

It's All About the Girl Group

We're five women in our thirties, unmarried and unencumbered by mortgages, car payments, or children, with our butts in the air, doing what is called, in yoga parlance, the downward dog. My actual dog, Bouckie, is lying on the carpet watching us. He lets out a yawn. We're listening to electronica music, a CD called *Drum and Bliss.* The windows are open, the sun is still out, and spring is seeping into our clothing. We breathe deeply as Tania leads us through our final asanas. We've taken to doing a little stretching before we start our girl-group meetings, although not without resistance from the peanut gallery, that is, everyone but Tania. We feel sort of stupid and ashamed at how New Agey we've become. After all, one of the things we share is a past fraught with ironic detachment and bad-girl cynicism. We spent our early twenties living typical

The connections between and among women are the most feared, the most problematic, and the most potentially transforming force on the planet.

—ADRIENNE RICH, *from* Disloyal to Civilization

bohemian existences, blasé and against everything and anything mainstream, only to then spend our late twenties and early thirties in therapy trying to figure out why we were always so pissed off. Now, older and apparently wiser, we're making fart jokes.

From 1999 to 2001, this group was my weekend date. Instead of spending our time mixing with our fellow *youngish* New Yorkers at rock shows, art openings, or other fabulous downtown happenings, my four friends and I sat in my apartment nibbling on crackers and cheese, sipping wine and sharing cigarettes, every Friday night for two years. The idea was to come together as women and artists (defined in the loosest way possible). Everyone in our group wanted to live artistically but wasn't exactly sure what that looked like. There was Tania, an actress and yoga instructor; Virginia, a public radio producer; Kate, a filmmaker; Cynthia, a painter; and me, a writer and crafty lady. We kept our structure fairly *un*structured: Sometimes we did yoga, sometimes we listened to a certain song or even meditated together (om shanti). After this, we would go around and give the update on our particular projects, be they student loan applications or writing film scenes. Thrown in the mix were details about our lives—the men we were dating, the bosses we hated, or, in my case, the wedding I was planning. Together we read self-help books, covering the book jackets with brown paper (God forbid anyone caught us reading something as dorky as *Eight Weeks to Optimum Health* or *The Money Drunk* on the subway). But mostly we ate, for no gathering of women is complete without food. There were giant strawberries, hummus, cheese, crackers, grapes, and, of course, chocolates, easy food that could be passed and consumed in between the stories we told each other about our lives.

Although it was merely five women sitting around talking and bending ourselves into uncomfortable positions for two hours a week, it was truly life-changing. I knew when we got together, I could let my veneer of competency and "having it together" slide, like kicking off a pair of high heels after a long night out. For a few hours each week, I didn't have to be the star employee or the joyous bride-to-be or the girl with the witty one-liner. Instead, I could be the woman who felt overwhelmed by the stresses of the workplace, conflicted about marriage, and just plain worn out. Of course, with these ladies I also could be ecstatic about the short story I had written or elated when I looked into my partner's eyes and felt his love and acceptance. On a good night, in our girl group, it was okay to just be.

And you know what? The time and energy we invested in listening and supporting one another paid off. With our help, Tania embarked on a Ph.D. in psychology, Virginia applied and was accepted to a prestigious urban studies fellowship, Cynthia started showing her paintings at galleries, Kate finished a screenplay after years of fitful starts and stops, and I found an ideal part-time job as a Web producer on a women's public radio program.

I don't know if we would have accomplished these things had we gone about them alone. Left to our own devices, most women I know, especially early in their careers or crafty lives, can think of about a million reasons why we shouldn't try anything new. That's where the group came in. Whenever one of us had doubts and wanted to give up, we were there to encourage her, like the perky blond cheerleaders we hated so much in high school.

Sadly, our Friday night girl group eventually broke up. I suppose it was inevitable. With all of our successes, we didn't need one another in the same way anymore. Two of our members moved out of state for their schooling, and the rest of us went our own ways on divergent paths. But we still find support in each other's company through late-night phone calls and the occasional get-together when one of the out-of-town ladies comes to New York for a visit.

So what does this group have to do with the crafty life? *Everything*. When we choose to live our lives consciously, to become creators, not mere consumers, sticking with it takes the support of other people who are doing the same. It takes courage to try new things, whether it is cooking an elaborate dinner for friends, trying a difficult knitting pattern, or exploring a different career path. It is risky to sit down and think about what *you* really want your life to look like. It might disappoint your parents, your boss, your lover, or your friends. It might go against what you're *supposed* to do. But I think it's worth upsetting a few people to live a joyous life. In our culture, the default position is to stick with what you've got, to settle. Work your job, go shopping at the mall, and eat Lean Cuisines every night for dinner, while zoning in front of the TV. Just don't ask for or want too much. If you want adventure, watch *Survivor.* If it's human connection you seek, tune in to *The View.* If you yearn for a decent government, don't organize or even vote, just watch *The West Wing.*

If you want to lead a more creative, crafty life, you need to build communities of resistance. If most Americans are passively living their lives, in order to craft yours consciously, you've got to get support, to surround yourself with others who are doing the same. For every risk I have ever taken in my life, there have been at least three people who have tried to discourage me. Their voices sounding like an alarm in my head: *A feminist craft site? No one will get it. Write poetry? You're too old. Work three days a week? You'll never be able to survive.* These voices were always wrong. Thankfully, I had enough crafty folks in my life who helped me see these messages for what they are: other people's fears.

In order to live a life not controlled by fear and passivity, we must surround ourselves with creative, risk-taking, crafty individuals. For me, these people are most often women. Whether it's a planned weekly girl group or just having my girlfriends over for beauty farm—an evening devoted to mud masks, toenail polishing, and other delightful feminine activities—I need to spend time in the company of women. I need to revel in women's culture, be it beauty, domesticity, or feminist theory.

When I am in the company of other women, I tend to feel better about what it means to be a member of the second sex. There is so much in our world that tells women we are less-than. Madison Avenue tells us we aren't of value unless we are sexy sixteen-year-olds. Intellectuals tell us if we care about what makes us beautiful, we are stupid, and only pursuits of the mind are worthy. The professional world tells us that our past history of domesticity and child rearing is unimportant. In some circles men and marriage are considered déclassé, and on the playground moms often shake their heads at our ambition. No matter what we do, we can't win. But when I'm with my crafty ladies, I can let some of that slide. I can talk about recipes I love or a pair of suede mules that make me really happy without feeling stupid—just as easily as I can plot my career advancement or feel proud of my marriage. I can listen to my friends and their fears or their accomplishments and have an open heart. Mostly I can practice being supportive of all the different choices women make and not belittle those decisions. So when Virginia had the opportunity to start a community radio station in Afghanistan, our girl group could help her pack up her apartment, not question her sanity.

And that's what so powerful about girl groups. Instead of women fighting over our limited slice of the proverbial pie—for who among us hasn't been saddened by the amount of female competition in the world?—we work to support one another, *even when we are jealous and don't feel like it.* If someone lands a killer job, we may feel a bit competitive about it, but we don't take it out on our friend. We can, if appropriate, say, "I feel jealous that you are getting what you want, but I'm also happy for you and proud that we've been able to help you get there." Because the group has been a part of the process, everyone can share in the glory. By including other people in the way we live our lives, we don't have to feel so isolated and alone, and we can share the good things that happen. When we come together as women, it's powerful, in a very real, feminist way.

That said, girl groups don't need to be all women (although, if this is the case, you might want to call it something other than a

Practically everyone now bemoans Western man's sense of alienation, lack of community, and inability to find ways of organizing society for human ends. We have reached the end of the road that is built on the set of traits held out for male identity—advance at any cost, pay any price, drive out all competitors, and kill them if necessary.

—JEAN BAKER MILLER, *from* Toward a New Psychology of Women

girl group) or consciously constructed as support vehicles. Simply building communities around things that you love to do is enough. When we make plans to try out a new restaurant together as part of a dining club, it forces us out of our homes and turns us on to new things and new ideas. When we start a weekly craft club at the local coffee house and make stuff together, we get inspired to create even more things. When we join a book club, we have a greater impetus to read books we might not have otherwise and to discuss ideas, rather than watch other people talk on TV.

Human beings are social animals. We are not meant to live isolated lives, but instead to live in communion with others. Sure, being part of a community is often a pain in the neck—people are messy, we say mean things, we don't share responsibilities equally, we complain, we get into arguments, and even when we work hard to make things equitable there's always someone who doesn't want to share—but it's better than the alternative: alienation and loneliness. By coming together, even with all the yucky stuff that goes along with intimacy, we have more than if we go about and through our lives solo. Once our society was organized around church and patriarchal family units. I don't know about you, but I don't want to go back to that world. I want to move forward with a ragtag army of nutty women (and men) who, even with their limitations, band together and dare to have more.

Quiz: Which Girl Group Is Right for You?

I believe there is always space in your life for community. The trick is finding the best group to fit your needs. If you work long hours, an evening dining club may appeal. If you are undergoing a major life transition, you might want something more focused on your personal growth. If you need to get fit, an exercise group could be nice. Starved for intellectual stimulation? A book group might be up your alley. Want to make the world better? Organize a Craftivism group. The possibilities are endless. To help you focus on your goals, I've designed this simple quiz.

- -

1. Would you describe yourself as:
   a. Going through a major life change (either starting a new career, ending a relationship, deciding to be an artist, etc.).
   b. Mostly happy with how things are but could always enjoy more social time.

2. How would you characterize your free time?
   a. What free time? Between friends, family, and work, I am booked.
   b. Plentiful. I am looking for a hobby or organization to bring meaning into my life.

3. The last time I exercised was . . .
   a. I can't remember that far back.
   b. Yesterday.

4. When someone name-drops a great book, you . . .
   a. Feel regret that you don't read more.
   b. Roll your eyes and think: "What an idiot!"

5. The following phrase describes my living situation:
   a. It's just me, myself, and I.
   b. Very populated.

6. Do you like to knit?
   a. Yes
   b. No

7. When Halloween comes around, do you . . .

    a. Work for weeks sewing your costume and bake spooky treats for your annual party?

    b. Turn out the lights and pretend you're not home?

8. When something has to be planned, are you

    a. The first person people call?

    b. The last person they think of?

9. Do you read restaurant reviews?

    a. Yes

    b. No

10. Finish this sentence: If I had more time and discipline I would . . .

ANSWERS:

1. If you answered:

    a. Sounds like you could really benefit from a weekly girl group designed to support your doing new things, like applying to graduate school, writing a resume, or starting to date again.

    b. A group that brings more joy into your life could be perfect for you. Maybe it's as simple as throwing a party or attending a stitch-n-bitch. If you like reading, a book club could work as well.

2. If you answered:

    a. A low-stakes group could be good for you. I recommend a one-time event, like a spa party. A well-established book club could work as well.

    b. You are blessed with free time. Why not organize your own group? You could throw a monthly clothing swap, knit for charity, or start a cooking club.

3. If you answered:

   a. An exercise girl group that meets a few times a week for running, swimming, walking, or yoga could really motivate you to take care of yourself. Heck, even a once-a-week girls' soccer game could be helpful. You might try posting a notice at your local gym or yoga studio for workout buddies. Make sure to include fun excursions to healthful restaurants or local hiking trails to keep it interesting.

   b. Even if you could pass for Xena's younger sister, exercising with others still could be enjoyable. You may want to plan a running or skiing date with a few friends.

4. If you answered:

   a. The book club is for you. It's a great way to discover new writers and build community at the same time. Plus, it will help you make time for reading.

   b. If you read a lot, or not at all and are happy with this fact, a book club still can be a great place to discuss ideas in a relaxed, nonacademic setting.

5. If you answered:

   a. Living alone doesn't always offer many opportunities for eating with others. If you enjoy making meals, a cooking club that meets on a regular basis could be ideal.

   b. If you live with your family or a bunch of roommates, you might enjoy getting away. A dining club that focuses on a new restaurant each month might be nice.

6. If you answered:

   a. If knitting rocks your world, a stitch-n-bitch is the group for you. Besides hanging with like-minded folks, you can ask for advice from more advanced knitters and show off your latest yarn achievements.

   b. If you don't like to knit but like hanging out with crafty people, you can always join a stitch-n-bitch and mend clothes, draw, or just drink coffee! Most knitters don't seem to mind having hangers-on.

7. If you answered:
   a. If you like to throw parties, by all means, do so and do it often. Any excuse works: a new job, a birthday, a random holiday, the first snow, or even a new tattoo.
   b. If throwing or even attending parties is not your thing, quieter social occasions may work for you. Simply going to a yoga class could satisfy your need for community. If you like to knit, a stitch-n-bitch, where folks aren't required to socialize, could work as well.

8. If you answered:
   a. You are someone who makes things happen. So do the world, or at least the less structured among us, a favor and organize your own girl group.
   b. You are always misplacing things and showing up late. Best you join an established group. You can contribute to the health of the organization by bringing treats or giving members a ride.

9. If you answered:
   a. Although you might not like the moniker, let's face it, you're a foodie. A dining club that explores the culinary world could be the community you've been searching for.
   b. Even if food isn't your thing, a cooking club might turn you on to a few easy recipes you could make for yourself, friends, or your family.

10. This final question is really the most important. If there are things in your life, like getting a new job or getting fit, that you've been putting off, a girl group can help you make a change.

Starting Your Own Girl Group

So you know four to six women who have similar goals, whether it is learning to cook, starting a new career, or learning a new craft, and you decide that you want to form your own girl group. Here are a couple of suggestions to get you started.

- *Decide on a meeting place.* You can rotate houses and the responsibility of hosting, or you can choose one woman's home and take turns providing food and drink. You can even find a regular meeting place like a café or restaurant.
- *Find a time to meet.* This is the hardest part of forming your girl group: deciding on a time and sticking to it. I highly recommend a regular time and day—for instance, every Tuesday at 7:00 P.M. or the third Sunday of every month.
- *Take turns producing the meeting.* One person always should take responsibility for sending out a reminder e-mail and organizing the meeting, even if it is at a café or restaurant.
- *Consider using an outside guide for structure.* My Friday Night Girl Group was started with the book *The Artist's Way* as our resource. Each week we read the chapters and did the exercises. The book gave us a way to organize ourselves, even if our discussions didn't always stick to the text.
- *Make time for a "business" meeting.* Every few months or so, it's a good idea to talk about how things are going. Maybe people would prefer meeting earlier or less regularly. A change of location may be in order. It's important to set aside time to discuss these details.
- *Be okay with changes.* Groups have a shelf life. They work for a while and then they stop. After a few years you may find people keeping missing nights, or it becomes impossible to get together. Instead of getting mad at one another, take the care to end the group on a positive note.

Starting a Stitch-n-Bitch

Knitting with other people is a great way to spend an evening. Most successful stitch-n-bitches are rather loose affairs, organized at local cafés, with a come-one, come-all attitude. Sometimes there are two knitters, sometimes twenty, depending on schedules and weather. On a good evening, there is a healthy exchange of knitting advice and gossip. If you are interested in starting a stitch-n-bitch, I recommend finding a local café or bar that will host a weekly knitting circle. Talk to the owners or managers first; most likely they will welcome the club on a slow night of the week. Now you have a location and a time. Next, get the word out about the group. You can make flyers to put up at yarn stores, local colleges, or even your favorite rock club. Then all that's left for you to do is show up each week. Simple.

Naked Lady Party

A fun way to build community is to host a Naked Lady Party. The idea is basic: A number of women get together to swap their stuff. The skirt that you wore every day all summer long and would puke if you had to wear just one more time becomes another woman's cherished item. Your dad's old sweater that sat in your closet for ten years collecting dust is taken by someone with plans to transform it into leg warmers through felting and sewing.

Rules of the road:

- Keep your invites down to ten or less. More gets chaotic.
- Make sure you choose a space that is large and airy, so

everyone can spread out. It should also be private, since you will be in various states of undress.

- Be supportive of everyone. Pay lots of special attention to creating a noncompetitive environment. Compliment each other and refrain from negative comments.

- Serve snacks. A bunch of hungry women and a pile of clothes could be a lethal combination.

- Don't be afraid to ask for what you really want, even if your best friend wants it too. However, if she looks really great in it, you should let it go. Be nice—there are plenty of clothes to go around if you have these parties regularly enough.

Here's how you might organize the swapping:

STEP 1: SORT

Dump everyone's clothing in the middle of a large room. Then sort all the clothing into categories: pants, dresses, shirts, outerwear, sweaters, shoes, and miscellaneous (belts, hats, purses).

STEP 2: AUCTION

After you sort everything, have one of the ladies "auction" off each item, holding it up for everyone to see, describing the size, fabric, brand, and other redeeming qualities. For instance: "This lovely 1960s housewife muumuu is acid orange and red, a size 8, polyester and cotton, and it's made by Hawaiian Island."

Then each member of the party raises her hand to make a "bid" (which of course is not a cash bid, but a show of interest). If there is more than one taker, you go into selection mode. Each girl who wants the item tries it on for the group—and after thoughtful comments have been made, if two or more still want the item, a vote is held. The bidders close their eyes and the team votes with a show of hands on which lady should get it.

Step 3: Trade

Once everyone acquires her loot, allow some time for additional trading or swapping to occur. It's important for everyone to have the opportunity to rethink her goods. If you like the tangerine head scarf that I got, you could offer me the 1970s fake Gucci bag for it. Or maybe you decided that you really don't need those purple satin pants, after all, but you've got to have that hair crimper.

Step 4: Thrift It!

Inevitably, you will have leftovers from your party—the Clue board game with missing pieces or the dirty shirt in size extra large with a plumbing logo on it that no one wanted. These items should be bagged and sent over to the local thrift store. If you are throwing a party, you should ask one of the participants to take responsibility for doing this.

Please feel free to come up with your own rules for your Naked Lady Party. Any way you organize it, I'm sure it will be great!

Beauty Farm

My friend Cynthia came up with this idea for a celebratory night of beauty treatments. I never quite understood why she named it Beauty Farm, but the name stuck and now I throw a Beauty Farm once every few months to indulge in girly splendor with my friends.

Here are a few tips to organizing your own Beauty Farm:

- *Be selective.* Invite three or four women over to your house who will most likely get along with one another. Political disagreements and interesting personality combinations that can be stimulating at a dinner party are just plain exhausting when you're half dressed and covered in odd creams and jellies.

- *Make contact through snail mail.* You might consider splurging on handwritten notes inviting your friends to attend. Who can resist a pink envelope that smells like perfume, especially when it holds an invitation to something called a Beauty Farm?

- *Be nocturnal.* My friend Emma has a fabulous Scottish mom named Nancy who married a rock star and managed to be both a mom and a hipster her entire life, without ever embarrassing her children. (How come we never hear about these types of cool women? It seems they only make headlines when they become drug addicts.) When we were teens, Nancy told us this great story about how, when she was in her early twenties, living in Glasgow, she would go out every night of the week but Wednesday. On Wednesday evening, she would paint her nails and wash her hair and do a bunch of beauty treatments. Her story inspired me to throw Beauty Farm at night, making it more of an affair than an afternoon would allow.

- *Make it BYOT.* To ensure the greatest variety of beauty treatments, ask each lady to bring one or two of her favorite masques (spelled the fancy way, of course), toners, creams, or nail polish. She also should bring a headband to keep her hair back, a washcloth, and a towel.

- *Creating the vibe.* Personally, there is nothing more appealing than the concept of a spa. Days spent getting massaged, being served healthful, delicious food, and taking dance and yoga classes—what could be better? Because we all can't afford to go to the spa on a regular basis, I try to emulate the experience during Beauty Farm by lighting lots of candles, burning calming essential oils like lavender, and playing soothing music, so everything smells and looks relaxing. I want my ladies to feel pampered and indulgent. I also like to offer a healthful spa menu of treats and finger foods and yummy nonalcoholic drinks.

PUTTING TOGETHER YOUR BEAUTY FARM MENU

Keeping with the spa vibe, you may want the menu light and healthful. Some suggestions include: multigrain bread with olive tapenade; grilled chicken breast, placed on skewers and served with a spicy peanut sauce; carrot sticks with hummus dip; steamed asparagus spears and brown-rice sushi rolls. For dessert, you might serve a low-fat angel food cake and fresh berries. Be creative: Any light, fresh, healthful finger foods will do. Beverages might include cucumber water (simply place slices of cucumber in a large pitcher of ice water; the result is a surprisingly refreshing drink), sparkling mineral water, or even fresh fruit juices. Try to avoid sodas or overly sugared or alcoholic drinks. Just remember, you want everyone to feel good and energized the next day, as if they had jetted off to La Costa for the evening.

Here are the things you'll need to provide:

> Nail polish remover
> Basic face soap
> Cotton balls
> A good basic astringent, preferably with witch hazel
> A good basic face moisturizer
> A thick moisturizer for hands and feet
> Food and drink: See my suggestions above.
> Girly movies: *Pretty in Pink, Breakfast at Tiffany's*, or episodes of *Buffy the Vampire Slayer* and *Sex and the City* are always good choices.
> Raw ingredients for the Make Your Own Beauty Treatments (see next page)

Make Your Own Beauty Treatments

If you are feeling very industrious, you and your ladies may want to create some of your own beauty products to be used during Beauty Farm. The following are simple spa treatments using all-natural ingredients.

OATMEAL, ALMOND, AND LEMON FACE SCRUB

This face scrub rivals those found at fancy day spas in New York City. Oatmeal works as a gentle cleanser, almonds are good for clearing out blackheads, and lemon zest has an astringent effect on the skin.

4 tablespoons oatmeal flakes

4 tablespoons finely ground almonds (Make this by throwing whole almonds in the blender and grinding on low. Just make sure you don't overgrind and make almond butter.)

4 tablespoons lemon zest (about 2 small lemons)

2 tablespoons water

Scrubs 4 to 5 faces.

Mix all ingredients in a medium-size bowl. Massage into skin, taking 2 to 3 minutes to really scrub out the dirt, going in a circular motion and avoiding the delicate eye area. Rinse with warm water and pat dry.

HERBAL STEAM TREATMENT

Steam cleans out your pores and gives you that I-just-got-a-facial look.

3 tablespoons fresh or dried herbs (chamomile, lavender, and/ or rosemary)

Creating a home steam is simple: Just heat a large pot with water on the stove. Once water is boiling, add herbs and turn off the heat. Then sit with your face at a comfortable distance from the steam—close enough to be warm but not hot—and place a towel over your head with the edges draping down past the pot to build a tent of steam. Stay above the pot for 3 to 5 minutes, then rinse your face with cold water and gently towel dry. Before the next gal steams, you'll want to boil the water again.

CLEANSING MASQUE TREATMENT

Honey removes impurities from below the skin's surface and clears away those pesky dead skin cells, which make your skin seem dull.

Scrubs 4 to 5 faces.   1 cup honey
                          ½ cup almond or olive oil

In a large bowl, combine the honey and oil until fairly well blended. Then each lady should apply enough to cover her face, being careful to avoid the area around her eyes. Spend 2 to 3 minutes massaging the honey-oil mixture into the skin, then leave the masque on for about 20 minutes. Remove with warm water and a washcloth. Pat skin dry.

Hint: You also can make the masque in a plastic tub with lid; simply shake well to mix the ingredients. The masque will last four weeks, sealed and refrigerated.

The Theme Party

What better way to feel connected than to throw an all-out bash, where friends of friends can get to know one another, talk, eat, dance, and have fun. One of the keys to throwing a killer soirée is coming up with a theme. The ladies of the community boards of getcrafty.com had a few ideas:

THE HEARTBREAK PARTY

Marisol, a bank teller from Arizona, came up with this brilliant party idea. She has her girlfriends dress up in thrift store prom dresses, listen to Johnny Angel–type songs, eat cupcakes, and talk about their heartbreaks.

PINK PARTY

Elizabeth from Tennessee loves pink and likewise is keen on throwing parties dedicated to this most wondrous of colors. She serves all-pink food—pink snowballs, pink champagne, and pink (beet) dip, and has all pink decorations. She also demands that all her guests wear pink. Those who don't obey are turned away at the door.

'80S PROM

Who wouldn't want to relive the feeling of slow dancing in a turquoise taffeta dress to "Don't You Forget About Me" by Simple Minds? Not Amy, from St. Paul, Minnesota, who pays homage to the era by throwing an '80s prom party. She plays '80s music, asks everyone to break out the old thrift store dresses, and then spikes the punch.

FAMILY RECIPE POTLUCK

Every family has one—a dish that is quintessential to their ancestors. It might be tacos or fried chicken or suet pudding or kim-chee, but it is something relatives enjoy year after year. At the Family Recipe Potluck, Tracy from Bellingham, Washington, asks all her friends to make and bring these family heirlooms. If nothing else, they are great conversation starters.

DAY OF THE DEAD

This wonderful holiday, which falls on November 2, is a Mexican ritual that celebrates those who have gone to the other side. Hammie likes to celebrate the Day of the Dead with her friends by decorating her home in flowers and candles, and building shrines to those who have passed. Other traditional ways to celebrate include serving the deceased's favorite foods and, of course, drinks.

CRAFTIVISM

The following groups offer crafty ladies the opportunity to build community through crafting.

- *The Church of Craft.* With chapters in Seattle, New York, San Francisco, Montreal, Stockholm, Los Angeles, and Toronto, the church sees making things as spiritual practice. It has no doctrines or ideology or rules; people just get together and craft. They knit sweaters, build tables, and sew skirts in community with one another. The Toronto chapter sums it up best when they say, "We're a small grassroots crafty collective rebelling against the culture of mass production. Not only are the things we create our own, but in this glossy, fabricated world, the simple act of creation is transcendent." Their Web site offers info on joining local chapters or starting your own: http://www.churchofcraft.org.
- *Revolutionary Knitters.* This group mixes politics and knitting. Revolutionary Knitters get together regularly to focus on animal rights, social injustice, and environmental issues, and, of course, to knit. You can start your own chapter or join an existing one: http://knitting.activist.ca/

CRAFT YOUR LIFE

Thank you for taking the time to read *Get Crafty.* I hope I inspired you to look at the domestic arts in a fresh, new way. But more important, I hope you walk away with the idea that when it comes to being crafty, it's not *what* you do but *how* you do it.

What I mean is this: Being crafty is not necessarily about knitting complicated sweaters or cooking elaborate feasts. It's about taking time to enjoy yourself and making something from nothing. It's about the process, not the end product. It's about viewing your whole life as one big craft project.

This is especially true when we widen the crafty philosophy to incorporate a new way of life for women, one that combines our past history as homemakers with the career and leadership opportunities we've fought for. In essence, this is what the New Domesticity is all about. It's about having it *all,* but redefining what the *all* is. It's about combining work and home and creativity and family and joy in a way that works for each individual woman. It's about throwing out the rules and refusing to get caught up in labels like "stay-at-home mom," "housewife," "career woman," "feminist," and "artist." It's about treating your life as a work in progress.

As women who demand to be respected as fully human, whose ideas, values, and history are not diminished, we are always in the process of figuring out who we are and what we want to be. When we craft our lives, we focus on growing and changing, not on being perfect. We learn to become experts at the art of improvisation and mixing and matching until something feels right. When it stops feeling good, we reorganize.

Part of crafting your life is not getting caught up in all the *shoulds*. If you don't want to bake muffins, then, by all means, don't bake muffins. We all have different needs and constraints on our lives; what works for one doesn't necessarily work for another. The New Domesticity movement acknowledges this. It's not about having immaculate floors or making your pasta from scratch (unless that floats your boat); it's about thoughtfully and consciously living your life and respecting the rights of other women to do it differently from you.

Crafty ladies organize their lives in myriad ways. Here are just a few examples from my own circle of friends, women who inspire me by the thoughtful way they juggle it all.

My friend Virginia lives alone in Boston and works as a radio producer. She gets crafty by putting together beautiful outfits, making her bed each and every day, and buying herself flowers. Cooking is not her thing, but she loves to eat well. She is part of a meditation circle and regularly goes out to listen to live music.

Lisa, a single mom who makes and sells soap out of her basement in Nyack, New York, gets crafty in a totally different but equally enjoyable way. She cooks dinner for her daughters each night from all-organic ingredients, buys only used clothing, and is part of a farming collective. She also creates decorative toilet seat covers, rides a motorcycle, sports many tattoos, and curses like a demon.

Julie is a corporate lawyer and a mother of three daughters. The four ladies live in New York City with the girls' dad, a university professor. During the day, the girls go off to the apartment of another mom whose kids are grown, and at night, their dad picks them up and makes them dinner. Julie works long hours. She gets crafty by baking cakes with the girls on the weekends, buying them lots of costumes for dress-up, and being an active member in her Quaker community.

For Susan, who lives in Portland, Oregon, with her boyfriend, working part-time is a key element to crafting her life. Although she doesn't have much money, she has plenty of time for sewing, knitting, cooking, and making beauty products. She organizes a stitch-n-bitch and is active in local politics.

I offer these examples not as models of perfection, but rather to show that despite their *imperfections*, despite their time, relationship, and money constraints, these ladies make room in their lives for joy and creativity and human connection. The truth is that if you wait until your life is more settled or you're less stressed or more financially solvent to craft your life, you will be waiting forever. The time to get crafty is right now. I wish you happiness and hope you can create your own way each and every day.

Jean Railla

Index

About the Author

JEAN RAILLA is the founder of getcrafty.com and a regular contributor to *Bust* magazine. She lives in Greenwich Village with her husband and son—and a closet full of unfinished craft projects.